CW00685785

THE SMART ONE

THE SMART ONE

David Ward

Book Guild Publishing
Sussex, England

First published in Great Britain in 2010 by
The Book Guild Ltd
Pavilion View
19 New Road
Brighton, BN1 1UF

Typesetting in Garamond by
Norman Tilley Graphics Ltd, Northampton

Printed in Great Britain by
CPI Antony Rowe

A catalogue record for this book is available from
The British Library

ISBN 978 1 84624 404 9

'If everything seems under control, you're just not going fast enough.'

Mario Andretti

Contents

Prologue

Motor racing is not for the faint-hearted. I love cars, I love speed, I love life in the fast lane but The Cannonball Run was so out of my league the thought of winning never entered my head.

I still don't know why I entered; the copious amounts of Kronenbourg lager one night probably.

Mentally I was mad enough for The Cannonball. Any bad behaviour on my part would be offset by the sober nature of my co-driver, Adrian Hull. He's a number-cruncher, an accountant, and that's as far as our qualifications for the race went.

I knew we would be outclassed.

Professionally I was up against some of the top drivers on the planet and some who *thought* they were the top drivers on the planet. The nearest I had ever been to winning any type of race was at my Tesco supermarket, heading towards the checkout with a trolley-load of booze. And if that didn't spell certain failure, the vehicle I chose to race in The Cannonball would hardly stand a chance against the high-performance cars being flown in especially for the event – Ferraris, Lamborghinis, Porsches and BMWs.

I had entered an elf-like and very huggable Smart car, and its finely tuned 700cc engine was certainly no match for the 2-, 3- and even 6-litre brutish powerhouses of the competition.

For a million drivers worldwide – including Joanna Lumley, star of *Absolutely Fabulous* – the Smart car is their car of choice. But not for a 3,000 mile, gruelling, three-country, European Cannonball Run. That, some would say, would be madness, a total waste of time. But then The Cannonball is almost a leap into motor racing insanity and, as I have just mentioned, I was well qualified for that, and maybe, just maybe, I had a teeny, weeny chance of finishing somewhere in the middle of the 38-car line-up and making a few bob for my favourite charity, the National Association for the Prevention of Cruelty to Children (NSPCC), at the same time.

Little did I realise the time had come for David to slay the Goliaths of The Cannonball.

My 20 minutes of fame was about to begin . . .

1

The Smartest Thing

My story begins as I was leaving the office.

'Take a look at this,' came the shout. Now normally, living in London all my life, I would do what every Londoner would do and totally ignore the request and carry on, or, if pressurised, retort with the obligatory volley of expletives which would question the parenthood of the person while telling them to go and fornicate, unless, of course, they were bigger than me.

This was no different, though here was a dealer. A dealer to my addiction, here was someone who saw the weakness in me and was ready to exploit it, as have the others – and yes there have been others, many of them! I turned and faced him and followed, knowing that I shouldn't. I wasn't ready to buy, I didn't need to buy, so what harm could it do me? Off I went down the ramp.

You see I have a weakness or addiction for cars. I can see good in every car apart from a Rover 75 – I'm not really sure what they have going for them, particularly as every one I see is normally some insipid colour, but then that's my view of them and, possibly, the worse thing I could say about a car. Now don't get me wrong, I'm not completely against Rovers – in fact I owned one, a 2.6 SDI which I took to Cornwall twice, where it broke down twice, the second time leaving me to literally fight my way through West London on Bank Holiday Monday in August by public transport. All seemed OK except that it was the last night of the Notting Hill Carnival before the 7 p.m. shut-down was introduced and with the Red Stripe, Malibu and all sorts all flowing, an eventful night was had by all thanks to 'Rover'.

I have owned well in excess of 60 cars and bikes and have been driving now for 29 years, covering about 20 countries in numerous vehicles, all of which I have loved and enjoyed but rarely kept for a long time. I'm just as happy in a £200 'smoker' as I am in a £50,000 Range Rover Sport (both of which I have owned). I can ride a Harley Davidson motorcycle with the same exhilaration as a Vespa scooter; similarly I get the same buzz out of a sports bike as I do from a weird looking customised vehicle – and yes, I have owned all of those also. Since moving into my most recent house three years ago I have entertained the neighbours with ten different cars. I've broken down in places that most people would squirm at the thought of. I've been that person who causes you to be late when you are desperate to get somewhere by blocking the one and only lane on a motorway or stalling and not being able to re-start the thing at a set of traffic lights. In fact I can confidently state that I've had more people laugh at me in a car than Russell Brand has had on stage. I have driven 60-odd miles with just one back brake, having snapped my brake pipes on a ridiculously lowered Morris Minor pick-up complete with go faster flames sprayed across the bonnet. I've broken down every 12 miles of a 200-odd mile round trip with a slightly bent distributor arm. I've had an engine fall out of a Talbot Solara (I kid you not) in London while Tottenham Hotspur fans were coming out of their ground (I support West Ham). The lowest Volkswagen Beetle in Essex, at one stage, was mine. I couldn't turn directly into a petrol station without scraping the bottom of the car. Similarly I couldn't get the thing through an MOT; but I still go on buying 'risks', as I like to call them, most recently a £300 Fiat Cinquecento from eBay, mainly due to the ultimate excitement of driving them. I know it sounds slightly strange but I still, when sitting in my car waiting for someone, play with the gears as if I'm driving, exactly as I did when I was a child in my dad's cars while I was waiting for him to finish work. I would mentally go through the gears as if the car was moving, changing up and down, indicating, overtaking, all in my head. To this day I can honestly say that the only test or exam I was ever desperate to pass was my driving test. No other test or exam has ever come close to that, even my motorbike test was a sort of 'turn up and see' affair, although I did pass that first time, as well as my driving test.

So back to my latest fix – and love of my life – a 'Fourtwo' Smart car 2002; white and black, the passion model, with electric wing mirrors no less. The first few days of driving were mixed with varying emotions ranging from 'Oh God is that someone I know? Hide!' to 'Look at me everybody! I've got a Smart car!' The car grew on me extremely quickly with its automatic and tiptronic gearbox, the easy driving position, the busy-ness of it all. The first example of how great these cars are came when parking. I saw the gap, a very small gap, and thought no way, but I also thought I would test it. The smallest gap in the world or so it seemed, but within seconds not only was I in and out again but had loads of room to spare! The thing when driving a Smart is that you are sitting at the back of the car, with no back seats and a tiny storage area as a boot and this gives you a false sense of size. I have put this to the test now numerous times in London, sometimes having to take my time as the spaces are getting smaller and smaller, and once or twice they have been too small: perhaps it's time to fit parking assist? Smart boast that they can park side on, which they surely can, however, what they forget to mention is that the doors are so bloody big that if two cars park too close either side then you're basically stuck outside your car, unless you're prepared to climb through the back window: and what with a lot of Smarts all looking the same that was another case for the magistrates and my lawyer.

Smarts are surprisingly sturdy and robust. They hold the road extremely well, which is certainly not how they appear to an outsider who hasn't driven one. The handling is extremely good, so if you ever find yourself following a Smart into a roundabout or bend at speed, be prepared for it to disappear because an experienced Smart driver won't be braking!

The strange phenomenon coupled with driving a Smart is that you appear to be the most courteous driver on the road. When seeing you approach people naturally think that you're going to let them out, and that's what they do – they pull out in front of you. It's at this point you do something once that you will never do again: beep the horn! You only do this once because when you do, half the population on the road, if they hear it, will instinctively look around for a 5-year-old on a tricycle, realise there isn't one, and point and laugh at you. While being laughed at you do two things: make a note to report that the horn isn't working properly and a further note to enquire how much privacy class will cost so that no one can see you!

However, the perkiness of the car, even though it's only 50hp, compensates for a lot of things – you do feel that the car offers a certain feeling of speed that belies the size of the engine and makes the transition from the freedom of a scooter to that of a car quite well. The quirkiness of the car soon grows on you and it rapidly becomes part of the family. As it has been launched in the USA, we will probably see on *Jerry Springer* 'I Married My Smart'! Two friends of mine, who also own Smarts, have the luxury of also owning a top of the range BMW and a Ferrari; however, they choose to use their Smarts daily rather than the other cars

I myself use the car every day and thoroughly enjoy everything about it. I wouldn't change a thing!

'What can I do to this to make it any quicker?' I asked this after a month or so of owning the car and 'not changing a thing'. Well, I have a legal and estate agency background, so changing my mind to suit is a 'compulsory occupational hazard'. I had decided that yes the car was quirky, yes it was fun, but still a bit slow. As with most things in East London, there's always someone who knows some-one who knows someone, and sure enough, enter 'smarts r us' ('srus'), a company in Nottingham who could make my Smart faster by 're-mapping' it.

Re-mapping, or 'chipping' a car involves using computer tech-nology to remove the speed restriction placed on the car by the manufacturer. A speed restriction is placed on the Smart at the outset to help it comply with the numerous restrictions pertaining to pollution and car tax costs. Down came the guy and 15 minutes later the car was done. I also added a K&N air filter and a chrome air intake. A few weeks later I went back for more and had the car lowered, an easy process of replacing the springs. This gives the car even more stability, making bends and roundabouts a sheer joy. It was now that the fun began with me, daily, frightening a whole host of hatchback and saloon drivers, generally pissing them off with a Smart car going too fast for them to overtake or having the indignity of being overtaken by one. Another friend of mine who owed a Brabus Smart refused to have his company livery put on it as, as he put it, the way he drives the car would cost him more customers than it attracted. I could see why. I was having a ball 'taking mine to Germany' and getting 80 to 85mph on the M11 autobahn plus blasting round the numerous country lanes of Essex and generally surprising a lot of people a lot of the time.

This was now the car for me. It is roomy, it can hold a set of golf clubs, it will do a million miles on a tank-full and it is surprisingly fast. Plus, it has a great little storage box in the dashboard which I discovered months into owning the car. Most people would have discovered this immediately, but I don't read the manuals and don't really look around the car, hence the late discovery of this extra treasure. Yes, this was *the* car. My decades of addiction had come to an end.

Barely a month after the discovery of the storage box, the car had been sold. I was off the wagon.

A phone call came in a Nottingham accent. 'I say old boy, a trusted colleague of mine has managed to procure a 2003 Brabus Smart from a lady owner. It's been re-mapped to 101hp. Can we interest you in this fine automobile?' (I am not very good at accents or impressions.)

Now working in sales I played my best negotiating skills and as quickly as the average heroin addict would say yes to a free trip to the poppy fields of Afghanistan I said yes. Ten days later I had sold my previous Smart and was picking up the new one from Nottingham. As I drove from smarts r us to the M1, I was, to be fair, a little disappointed. Firstly Nottingham is miles from East London, way past St Albans in fact, and secondly while the car was much sturdier and felt a lot more rigid it didn't seem much quicker than my previous one.

I settled back for the long drive to London, some 120 miles! Fiddling with the radio I found Talk Sport, but it was poor reception. Now mightily pissed off I came down the ramp to the M1 and instinctively thumped my foot to the floor. Up through the tiptronic gears I went, my dark mood gone in ten seconds – the thing was flying! My journey back to London was fantastic and while the Smart Brabus can't compete with the supercars, compared to my other Smart and lesser cars, it was brilliant. The look on people's faces when I passed them was fantastic, and is something that, even today, I have never got bored with. The small nagging idea of possibly doing The Cannonball in a Smart had begun.

2

Keep Your Mouth Shut in a Pub

Car dealers and estate agents are renowned for their honesty, temerity and in general are pillars of the community. When are you ever going to read that again? Throughout my adult life I have dealt with them on more than one occasion. I say this because later on both professions will feature in this book.

So how did the Smart car and The Cannonball come together?

It was at the time I was impersonating a 5-year-old on a tricycle hurtling around in the souped-up Smart when my attention was drawn to an extract on YouTube showing a Hayabusa-engined Smart car, 'the Diablo'. One thing led to another on the site and via the related links I found a clip of a car doing The Cannonball Run. A nice car, in fact, and so after Googling and Asking Jeeves, I discovered a lot more about the race. Sorry, 'rally'. To call it a race would make it possibly illegal, however an organised rally skirts round that avenue of law – apparently.

I thought, why not enter a Smart car, just as a novelty really, an adventure, a dare, and all because it is a brilliant car. However, this mad idea compounded into a definite promise as I stupidly said I would do it to liven up an incredibly boring night I was having in a pub with a couple of clients. I was already on a head-on collision with the Kronenbourg lorry that was hurtling toward me and with great gusto I proclaimed that I would be competing in The Cannonball Run driving a Smart car. A stunned silence fell in our circle.

'Why?' they asked.

Well, Kronenbourg made me do it, in reality, but I explained again that the car was brilliant and obviously different to probably every other car that would be entering. I left the pub feeling quite positive, pissed, well both. I would be doing the bloody Cannonball in a Smart car.

I have been quite lucky; I have acted on impulse and without thought on many occasions in the past, leading me mainly having to give thought as to how to get myself out of situations, rather than thinking about a situation before getting into it, which, consequently, has seen me give up two good and lucrative jobs and go travelling or studying, leading me into numerous adventures! I regret none of them apart from one: when in Australia, Melbourne in fact, staying at a backpackers in the late 1980s I failed to contact three Swedish girls who advertised for a man to join them travelling in their car across to Perth! And to this day I still wonder ... what car they had!

I left grammar school at 16 without an exam to my name, compounded due to the fact that the local paper used to publish the all the O level results for the year and my surname was sandwiched between Smith, ten O levels, and Whittle and Wiskin, about ten each, so my zero didn't look too good. The careers master was very well versed in accountancy, law, medicine and insurance broking (it was a grammar school after all), and was perplexed when I declared that I wanted to be an air steward. I was dispatched with a 'write to British Airways' and that was it. I did, and didn't get a job, so all was looking bleak at 16.

In a roundabout way I arrived at a firm of solicitors in the West End of London having been cruelly spurned by British Airways telling me I was too young at 16 to be part of the cabin crew. They suggested I get a job working with the public and that I reapply at 18. I would have had experience of working with said public and this would help me. It seemed a logical idea but what other possible job could I do? I wrote to Marks and Spencer requesting any Saturday jobs, as I did not want to face the public five days a week and perhaps a Saturday would be a great way to ease myself in gently until I was ready, or more importantly, the public was ready for me!

I didn't hear back from Marks and Spencer but curiously got a letter from this firm of solicitors. I finally opened the letter, having got my alibi straight, to find that it was a missive explaining that they didn't work Saturdays – well good for them, nor did I, in fact I didn't work any day of the bloody week, but why tell me? They went on to explain that there was a summer job available with them.

My careers master had addressed us, once, with a good bit of advice. 'Boys, in the summer holidays try to get some job interviews. Then, when you come to apply for a job interview when you leave school you will have some experience.'

Armed with this bit of advice I replied to the solicitors who informed me on the phone that they actually didn't have a summer job; they were now looking for someone permanent. So with the voice of my careers master ringing in my ears along with many a Sex Pistols and punk classic at the time, I told them that I had too changed my mind and that a permanent job was what I was looking for. Of course it wasn't, but a chance to have a job interview in readiness for the 'big one' at British Airways.

It was the luncheon vouchers at 25p a day being part of the job offer that swayed it for me; truth be known, the rest of the job description had been a blur, something about courts, clients, forms – all minor obstacles to getting £25 per week and 25p a day luncheon vouchers. I had travelled to Baker Street with no intention of getting the job, and I met a nice man called Mr Berry who explained what I would be doing, apparently, and finished with 'Did I want the job?' With the mouth-watering prospect of 25p a day for food I said yes and when asked if I had any questions I tactfully enquired where the sandwich bars and cafés were. I also told them I had taken six O levels and that I had always wanted to be a solicitor. It transpired that the original letter I wrote to Marks and Spencer in Baker Street London was mis-directed to the firm of solicitors, hence their letter to me.

I lasted four years at that firm and found that the hours I thought they originally told me were dwarfed by the actual hours I worked (I should have listened at the interview). However, I enjoyed the work but felt after four years that it was time to leave as the luncheon vouchers were being phased out. I departed to study car mechanics as by this time an addiction was raging. I was at fever pitch when *Exchange & Mart* came out, and at one stage, while still living at home, I owned seven vehicles. I have owned every type of Morris Minor apart from the traveller which, ironically, I used to get a lift in to the station in the mornings from a mate who lived round the corner from me and worked in the next street for the traffic wardens in Portman Place.

One of my claims to fame at this time was to buy a Ford Transit recovery van for about £220. I had only been driving it for about half an hour when it broke down in a main thoroughfare in East London on a Friday night in the rush hour. I was famous on the traffic reports that night! Having fixed the van, myself and my friends would have hours of fun pulling up at unsuspecting victims with the flashing lights on full and waiting for them to come charging out of their houses wondering what the hell was going on. Another of our 'pranks' was to cruise the lovers' lanes and lay-bys looking for couples. We would silently push our cars around the unsuspecting car and on a sign blast out Capital Radio's disco music that they played every Friday and Saturday night; at the same time as the music blared out we would flash our lights and sound our horns. Up popped the heads and another night was ruined for all those courting couples. We were so popular our exploits even made it to the local paper with the headline 'Disco Squad Strikes Again'.

I sold the van for £450 about three weeks later.

The only sour point when leaving the solicitors was that I was leaving at the same time as the senior partner was going on holiday – yes, my stature had grown so much that neither of us could have the same time off together! By day a respected advocate (of sorts), in my spare time I was a menace on the open road, driving an assortment of vehicles that included a Fiat 500, a Morris Minor convertible with a Riley 1500cc engine, a split screen Morris Minor van, a lowered and severely chopped Morris Minor pick-up, a 1275cc Minor saloon which was seen on *Top of the Pops* and *Saturday*

Superstore in a David Grant video, 'Rock the Midnight', an Escort estate, a 50cc scooter, and a black Mini Clubman with bucket seats, black windows and a hole in the exhaust that made it sound faster! Added to these were numerous rusty Fords and Fiats. We were not without the odd 'tuck up' against others and similarly against us. When selling the Fiat 500 we towed it to the guy's road and when my mate knocked on the door I gently rolled down the road and pulled up outside so it looked like we made it under our own steam. He handed over the money and off we went. We in turn bought a 'mint Volkswagen Beetle' that turned out to be anything but, and when carrying out a bit of spot welding the newspaper that in fact doubled as a wheel arch burst into flames, destroying the back half of the car. And so the scams and double-crossing went on and on.

The car mechanics course I attempted to enrol on after leaving the solicitors turned out to be too basic: as I could recognise a spark plug I was over-qualified. A year later, after bumbling through a technology course instead I decided to go back to work at a solicitors' practice in Camden. While working there I bought a TVR Tasmin and this car turned my head so to speak and began a 'new phase' of cars: the 'WAG' cars I call them. They were a high maintenance, but looked nice, drove nicely, you felt good in them, but equally it cost you a fortune to get rid of them! My car experience was stepping up further gears, culminating in a Renault Turbo 11 which I owned in the late 80s. This is the car that appeared in the James Bond film *Never Say Never Again*, driven by SPECTOR agent Fatima Blush. My car career took a nose-dive after selling the Renault when I bought a BMW 635csi which turned out to be the biggest WAG of them all. However, I was fortunately earning good money and it was the 80s. I left a job selling houses and flats – some people refer to this as estate agency, I like to think of it as a 'building logistics manager' especially when working in Chelsea and Kensington – so without a job and income the cars had to go. I compensated for this fact by going travelling around the world for a year.

I believe that if you are lucky enough to spend three weeks or more away from work or a normal routine, one of two things happen:

1   you hate it and immediately go back to your old routine, culminating in having a wife, kids, dog ,Volvo etc.

or

2   you love it and are the type of person who spends the rest of your life looking for or dreaming about the next trip, making them whenever you can.

I would class myself as most definitely a 'No. 2 type person'. Perhaps I should rephrase that: I would be in the second category, and that, in a huge M25 roundabout way brings me finally to set the scene concerning how I found myself doing The Cannonball Run in a Smart car but with whom?

3

Snow, Eyeliner and a Furious Italian

My hands were bloody freezing as the bumper slowly, very slowly, came off the Alfa – I think it was an Alfa. All I remember was the drive down to near Southend in Essex on a snowy, freezing Saturday in the very early 80s. I had somehow managed to get talked into spending a Saturday afternoon helping Adrian, a friend from school who was not in any of my classes except for sports as he was one of the clever ones, fix the bumper of a car that he had smashed into whilst driving either his Spitfire or Triumph Herald. He was a pseudo hairdresser at the time, and rather than claim on the insurance he took it upon himself to fix the bumper; why I was drawn into the whole thing, I don't know. Still, the Alfa owner was good enough to supply us with hot mugs of tea while we thrashed around with all sorts of strange spanners and sockets at the rear of his car, finally swapping over the old dented bumper for a shiny new one.

The very early 80s were exciting times – apart from lying in the snow in Southend – as is, I believe, any era when you are in your late teens and early Twenties. We had the benefit of the punk scene closely followed by the New Romantic era, which Adrian and I followed, although he was more into soul and jazz funk. However, our worlds crossed paths mainly through cars and following West Ham, who had at that time the distinction of being supported by two infamous gangs: the under fives and the ICF, who would regularly get coverage in the papers for their outlandish acts of violence and the way they terrorised other fans up and down the country.

Nowadays I can see why, as it would appear that every West Ham fan over the age of 35 claimed to be in the ICF which, theoretically, boosted the gang's numbers to about 800,000. I knew of the gang and in fact played Sunday morning football with a few of them for a pub called Queens in Barking in the East London and Essex league, but to say I was in the ICF would be lying, so I won't. I witnessed a lot of the trouble and on a few occasions came close to it smudging my blusher and ruining my eye liner - I was a New Romantic after all. When I wasn't charging around the UK following West Ham or dismantling Alfa bumpers, Saturdays and Sundays were spent dismantling Morris Minors and the like, particularly the last Saturday of the month, getting the cars ready for the Chelsea Cruise, magical nights cruising the Kings Road in Chelsea and circuiting Battersea Bridge and Albert Bridge, with a whole host of American cars, old Fords with V6 and V8 engines, model T Fords, a complete assortment of wild and wacky cars plus an eager and enthusiastic bunch of onlookers. Adrian's interest in cars again slightly differed from mine, he favouring the slightly older Triumphs, whereas I liked anything different. When our worlds crossed there would always be something that would happen; that's what makes me think there must have been a bigger reason I was freezing in Southend wrestling with a bumper.

The early years would see Adrian and me being pursued through Gants Hill station underpass by a group of skinheads and their Alsatians after trying to get in at the Tottenham and Aston Villa game that saw the debuts of Ricky Villa and Osvaldo Ardilles and which also saw half of London trying to get in to the ground; being caught in the Shed end at Chelsea in no man's land between West Ham and Chelsea fans, having minutes before been surrounded by the Chelsea 'boys' stating that "fuckin' West Ham are still in here". Yes we were, standing right next to you! I didn't say that at the time but chuckled it to myself. Orient FC, the nearest ground to where we both lived, also saw regular attendances from us with again little incidents and a couple of large ones at home to Ipswich, one of them being when Adrian decided to wear his West Ham scarf and stand with the Ipswich supporters. Ah, happy days. We were a rag tag group, one wearing a West Ham scarf and a few others looking like manic versions of David Bowie complete with eye liner and pixie boots,

On the way to the Blitz club in Covent Garden (the famous Steve Strange hosted club) one Tuesday night, dressed in the Robin Hood look, we had the misfortune to hit a cat that had run out in front of us. We were late, well I was late, and as I recall if you got there before 9 p.m., entrance was free – that was, of course, if Sir Strange let you in – and money being tight we always tried to get there before 9. Luckily the cat we hit just bounced off the car and survived. However, a woman who saw the incident was more shocked to see two Robin Hood-type characters getting out of the car to inspect any damage.

I was with Adrian when he managed to get run over by a Volkswagen Beetle in the mountains in Italy. We had gone there on a school skiing trip, but didn't restrict our activities solely to skiing. Apparently, the local shop reported a lot of items going missing, plus a girls' school at the same resort wasn't too enamoured with our intentions, their teachers getting in the queue rapidly forming to complain about us. We, as a punishment, were banned from skiing, allowing us to wander round the resort. This particular day, a snowball fight developed which involved most of those not skiing. Adrian was holding his own in the middle of the road, oblivious to a Volkswagen Beetle coming along it. A triple pike, double somersault and smashed windscreen later and we were confined to our hotel. Our adventures went on right up to him getting married. I subsequently moved up to Chelsea and plied my trade as an Estate Agent or building logistics manager while he stayed in Essex as an accountant.

Our paths still crossed, with cars and West Ham the two points of interest. I went away for just under a year, travelling (not 'going away. as in 'locked up in a tiny cell with a tiny transistor radio and a good mate called 'Bubba' who would keep you warm at night' way), returned to England, got married and had two boys. Adrian in the meantime stayed married, as he still is, and had two girls. My marriage didn't go the distance, as they say, so I was let loose again and, again, cars became a focal point, as well as attending the odd West Ham game along with 33,000 ICF members. The custom cars of the late 70s and 80s were replaced by souped and chipped up cars, not too visual but nevertheless still exciting to twenty-year-olds. But I still hankered after the older cars and Adrian had progressed to an E-type Jag.

2007 came and a conversation in the pub after a few of France's finest Kronenbourgs had left me in an embarrassing situation, but that's another story. It also left me trying to work out how the hell I had got myself into the position of claiming that I would do the Cannonball Run in a Smart car. Having accepted my fate and having to do it, I spoke to Adrian, who was really keen on the idea – his bravery (and foolhardiness?) surely knows no bounds. Here is one final story recognising the bravest man in Essex, if not the world:

In Epping in Essex, where Adrian now lives, there is a fish and chip shop. Many years ago we would often meet in Epping, go to a pub and then on for fish and chips. Amongst our friends was a legendary character who had a remarkable resemblance to the serial killer Fred West, except that he had a scar down his cheek, plus a look that could have bouncers apologising to him (yes it happened). One particular night, fuelled with drink, we headed to this fish and chip shop. In we went, about five of us, with this friend bringing up the rear. Crash! The plate glass window in the door smashed and this friend ended up standing at the front of the shop with shards of glass all around him. Silence fell over the shop for a second or two until my friend calmly said, "Portion of chips please, mate", totally oblivious to the damage he had caused.

Now in steps the bravest man in the world, confronted by a

manic Fred West lookalike covered in glass from walking through a plate glass window. He says,

"Oi mate, there's a queue here."

That incident really did sum up the times, the places, and our upbringing, so could the Cannonball compete?

So, in what is fast becoming the norm as The Police, Take That, Blur, Ultravox and, of course, Spandau Ballet stage their comebacks, two more massive icons of the 80s, David and Adrian, have reformed to bring you Cannonball 2008.

4

Cannonball

For me, films have always offered that 90 minutes-plus of escapism, allowing me to switch off and forget my problems, anxieties and stresses. Films have always played some part in the make-up of all our lives, inspiring us, upsetting us, making us laugh out loud and generally leaving us with thought-provoking ideas. We can all name our favourite films, and I'm sure that as you read this they immediately pop into your head. I would doubt that any of you have actually thought, 'Yes that *Cannonball* film is definitely my favourite, that bit when the weird doctor appeared from the ambulance, or wasn't Roger Moore brilliant in his role, we all know a Captain Chaos, and what actually happened to that Burt Reynolds?' No. I doubt any of you actually thought that did you, but the film must have left some sort of mark on you as for the sheer fact that you are reading this, which involves The Cannonball, so the thought must have been there (unless you are the type who spends hours in bookshops thumbing through books and have just happened to open it at this page).

Where did the film originate? A lot of films are adapted from books and make the transition from script to film badly. How many times have people said 'not as good as the book'. Equally, true-life events have often been transposed into film often suffering from a certain amount of 'exaggeration factor' to make the film more 'entertaining'! However, the *Cannonball* doesn't actually fall into either category and the whole car racing genre has overlapped with the film world numerous times. Where did it all start? Probably back in the 1930s, but I will come to that later. The 1970s produced

19

a whole host of recognised classics: *Star Wars, Saturday Night Fever, Jaws, Grease, Rocky,* and the period also supplied classic car films that any car buff would definitely rank in their top five. In 1971 *Vanishing Point* was released, starring Barry Newman and an awesome Dodge Challenger, in which Newman plays an ex-cop who gets 'into' car delivery. The film extensively involves him travelling from Denver to San Francisco in 15 hours and took a certain inspiration from the film *Easy Rider* but added a car with a maverick driver instead of a bike with a couple of maverick riders. People were still talking about this film when the second 'classic' hit the screen six months later, namely *Two Lane Blacktop* staring James Taylor and a brilliant Warren Oates playing a Walter Mitty-type character. This film centres around a duel between a 55 Chevy with its two free-spirited occupants played by Dennis Wilson and James Taylor, and a new 1970 Pontiac GTO driven by Oates. The film epitomises the care-free travelling life that surrounded road travel, with the constant stream of hitch-hikers picked up by the drivers during the race being a testament to that. The film emphasised this characteristic more than *Vanishing Point*. What *Two Lane Blacktop* also did was to inspire a certain Brock Yates into putting together the idea of a race.

At the time, Brock Yates was the editor of an American car magazine, *Car and Driver* and also did work as a pit reporter for CBS covering the NASCAR and in particular the Daytona 500. He became particularly busy in the early 1980s, writing several books and managing also to fit in writing a film, called *The Cannonball Run*. He also cites another main influence in addition to *Two Lane Blacktop*: Erwin G. 'Cannonball' Baker, who set numerous coast-to-coast records, the first being in 1914 when he drove an Indian motorcycle coast to coast in 11 days. His most famous run was in the 1930s when he travelled across the States in a Graham-Paige Model 57 Blue Streak 8 in 53 hours and 30 minutes at an average speed of 60mph, which, ironically, was a quicker average speed than that which was law – 55mph. In the 70s, when The Cannonball was first run, this run was also labelled as a demonstration against the draconian speed laws in force at that time, which were in fact put in place to combat a fuel crisis. Erwin's record time stood for nearly 40 years, and even more remarkable was that when the Run was recorded in 1933 there were no motorways built that covered the entire route.

The wheels of The Cannonball Run first began to turn in 1971 when Yates' son Brock Jr, friends Jim Williams and Steve Smith, plus Yates himself, in a Dodge Van called Moon Trash II, crossed the States not necessarily in a race but rather as a reconnaissance and fact-finding mission. Due to this first crossing there have often been disagreements as to how many Cannonballs have been run. If one was to include this then there were five, the second taking place later that year after the first year of races, 1971; the underground word was spreading and a movement of sorts was beginning to gather. A year later the next race, and in fact the most pivotal one of all, was building. The aim of the race was also becoming clarified and was defined as: 'The object of the Cannonball – Baker was to leave the Red Ball Garage on East 31st Street in New York, later a venue in Darien, CT, usually after midnight, and drive to the Portofino Inn in California in the shortest time possible'. Those were the only rules. Nothing was specified as to the route (ironically a dispute has arisen between the two drivers vying for the current record, Alex Roy and Richard Rawlings, as to the exact route), type of vehicle or maximum speed permitted. Speeding tickets received along the way were the driver's responsibility and would in general increase the car's overall time if stopped.

The Cannonball Run was technically a race in which the fastest time was declared the 'winner' and the results were announced in order of time, but times were not taken very seriously and it was found that sheer speed frequently did not guarantee a first-place finish due to delays by traffic police and more frequent stops for petrol and so on. Even by today's standards, while not as extreme as the tortoise and the hare analogy, a good average speed over the 3,000 miles will always beat the 'quick blast followed by quick blast' mentality.

The second race (the first proper one) took place in November 1971 with eight entrants and, as previously stated, was the race that brought the event to the public's attention. The race was won by Dan Gurney who won the 1967 24-hour Le Mans. He won the race in his Ferrari Daytona in a new record time of 35 hours and 54 minutes, averaging 80.80mph. His co-driver was Brock Yates. The race was reported in car magazines and press and received a positive 'spin'.

The Cannonball race history lists just a few accidents, involving a spilled pasta dish in a motor-home that cruised the route in approximately 57 hours, an all-female team who crashed their car near El Paso and didn't finish the race, and the worst crash of all, which occurred when a stretch limo catapulted off the road, breaking one on the occupants' arms. Incidentally, to date, the most serious accident in this type of road rally took place in 2007 when two Macedonians died as a result of a collision with one of the competitors driving a Porsche. This however was in The Gumball 3000 and not The Cannonball; nevertheless, bearing in mind the number of competitors in both The Cannonball and The Gumball, plus the other similar events throughout the year, the number of injuries is thankfully low, testament primarily to the organisation skills and driving abilities of the competitors.

The following two Cannonballs took place in 1972 and 1975 respectively. The first was won by another legendary figure at the time, Steve 'Yogi' Behr, driving a Cadillac in 37 hours 16 minutes and averaging 78.04mph. In 1975 the race was won by Jack May and Rick Cline in a 1973 Ferrari Dino 246GTS in a time of 35 hours 53 minutes with an average speed of 81mph. The last rally proved to be the most influential on Yates' writing. In April 1979, 46 cars left the starting grid situated behind the Lock Stock and Barrel club in Darien, Connecticut. This was by far the largest number of entrants, with 42 cars finishing out of the original 46. Seven of the cars actually completed without getting any speeding tickets while one car got five. Among the group were cars and characters that were later portrayed in the *Cannonball* film. A Rolls-Royce Silver

Wraith was brought over from the UK by Mr and Mrs Kendall-Lane, who not only brought their car but also a professional driver, a team of three relief drivers plus a whole wardrobe of outfits to wear, an ambulance complete with a 500bhp racing car engine, upgraded suspension and wide wheels, and a fully qualified doctor complete with an official-looking cooler bag containing a pig's heart. Other vehicles included a van mocked up as a US satellite detection unit complete with Geiger counter, a Ferrari capable of blacking out its rear lights if pursued at night and a van carrying 165 gallons of fuel to compensate for its mammoth 4.7mpg return. Interestingly enough, in this world of high fuel prices the most economic car on the 1979 Cannonball Run was a Lotus Esprit with 26mpg. While on the subject of fuel and payments, the second car to finish this race was a 6.9-litre Mercedes which finished eight minutes after the winner. It is said, that due to the fact that the driver of the Mercedes paid with a credit card at each petrol stop, the time taken to process the card was long enough to push the entrant into second place.

The last of the original Cannonball Runs was won by Dave Heinz and Dave Yarborough driving a Jaguar XJS who completed the distance in 32 hours 51 minutes, which equates to an average speed of 97.25mph with a fuel consumption of 12.5mpg. This time became the Cannonball record until 1983 when, during an independent race called The US Express, which was slightly longer than the Cannonball, the record was broken with a time of 32 hours 7 minutes. This held until 2006 when Alex Roy, a regular on the Gumball circuit, and David Maher, travelled the distance in 31 hours and 4 minutes; however, this record has been disputed by Richard Rawlings and Dennis Collins who covered, in their words, the 'correct route' in 31 hours 59 minutes. The dispute lingers on with Brock Yates refusing to be drawn on the subject. It would seem that in its original format the race was run in a celebratory happy state with the competitors continuing the feel and carefree ways of the 1960s; it is therefore symbolic that in the 2000s the once light-hearted aspect of the event has a commercial and serious cutting edge to it.

Back to the 1970s. James Taylor and Warren Oates are fighting it out over pink slips and a wayward girl who at the end of the film ended up on the back of a chopper, as in *Easy Rider!* The next car film that was released was *American Graffiti* in 1973, which incidentally used the same 55 Chevy which was used in *Two Lane Blacktop.* While this wasn't a road race film it did involve street racing and fuelled the fantasies of car fanatics hooked on the secretive street racing meets. This world is still evident today with car clubs up and down the country and late-night impromptu drag racing regularly taking place.

In late February 2008, news reached the public in the UK of a horrific car accident in Maryland, USA, where a crowd of 50 people were gathered and a car struck them, killing seven and injuring four. This happened in the early hours of the morning where there had been evidence of street racing. The modern film industry and Hollywood in particular has taken this brand of street racing and added their particular slant to it with the *Fast and Furious* films which, admittedly, probably appeal to the PlayStation and Xbox generation and are really considered laughable to any self-respecting 30-year-old-plus car fan.

The underground rumblings of The Cannonball Runs led to the 1976 release of *The Gumball Rally* in which the coast-to-coast race was again the main feature. Released in the same year was *Cannonball* also known as *Carquake*, both films loosely portraying events based on The Cannonball Run with *Carquake* adopting a darker, more destructive side, culminating in a mass pile-up while *Gumball* ended with a celebration. To this day these films still fuel rumours of illegal road races and associated characters still participating in underground racing in the USA. Of course today there is the larger commercial Gumball 3000 which has attracted extensive worldwide media and celebrity entrants. In fact 2008 saw the event start in the USA and end in China in conjunction with the Olympics, with the competitors having a stop-over in North Korea. Again drawing comparisons with the original Cannonball Runs, the modern day Gumball event is really out to court as much publicity it can and has done a good job; whereas the original Cannonballs were a private, mysterious affair with any publicity being hard fought if it was ever wanted in the first place.

In 1981, two years after the last Cannonball Run of 1979, *The Cannonball Run* hit the screens boasting a fantastic casting. The lead was taken by Burt Reynolds; however, he was not the first to be considered for the part: that honour went to Steve McQueen who unfortunately died before he could be formally asked. The film was written by Brock Yates and directed by Hal Needham (he of the ambulance fame in the 1979 Cannonball Run) who was a talented stuntman in his own right. The film boasted a cast that included Dom DeLuise, Roger Moore (while James Bond), Farah Fawcett, Dean Martin, Sammy Davis Jnr and a young Jackie Chan, to name but a few. Cameo roles were given to Brock Yates, Robert Tessier, Peter Fonda and the director himself. The car cast was equally impressive with Ferraris, a Lamborghini Countach, an Aston Martin DB5 (guess who drove that), a Rolls-Royce and a NASCAR Pro-am stock car.

So what of the finished product? The film was nominated for two awards: the Golden Screen Award (Germany) in 1985 and a Razzie Award 1982 (worst supporting actress Farah Fawcett). Brock Yates was said to be unhappy that the film was construed as a comedy when he wanted it to be a serious look at The Cannonball; however, he wasn't upset enough for him not to be involved in *Cannonball II* (1984) which he co-wrote with Hal Needham. This film retained a lot of the original cast but was generally panned, receiving no fewer than eight Golden Raspberry nominations.

In 1989, *Speed Zone* was released. It was whispered in close circles that it was *Cannonball III*, but it certainly wasn't – the only thing it really had in common with the previous films was a certain Jamie Farr, who appeared in the previous two and took the time to dust off the robes and play the Sheik Abdul Ben Falafel for a third time.

Realistically speaking, *Cannonball* theoretically ended in the mid-1980s as the last film in 1989 was far removed from the original and follow-up. Are we then expected to believe that, equally, the car fanatics who fed off the films or were lucky enough to take part just walked away from the whole thing? Rumours have persisted that legendary races continue to take place in secret.

With regard to the original races of the 1970s, Table 1 shows a list of the competitors prepared as best as possible with the information to hand.

Table 1

Last name	First name	Run	Time	Place	Vehicle	Year
Adamwitz	Tony	2	36.47	2	Chevrolet Van	1971
Adelbert	Harvey	5	36.19	9	Mercedes-Benz 300 D	1979
Alden	Al	5	32.59	2	Mercedes-Benz 450 SEL 6.9	1979
Allen	Gerald	5	36.20	10	Excalibur	1979
Ammerman	Craig	4	45.36	17	Travco Motorhome	1975
Arentz	Gary	5	39.10	19	Jaguar XJS	1979
Armstrong	Keith	5	39.20	20	Chevrolet El Camino	1979
Armstrong	Ted	5	39.20	20	Chevrolet El Camino	1979
Arutunoff	Anatoly	4	49.32	18	Bristol 410	1975
Arutunoff	Anatoly	5	40.33	24	Volvo 242 GT	1979
Atwell	Jim	4	38.56	7	Porsche Carrera	1975
Atwell	Jim	5	42.28	29	Porsche Carrera	1979
Baker	Clyde	3	41.15	13	AMC Hornet	1972
Baker	Terry	5	35.58	7	Ferrari 308 GTS	1979
Behr	Steve	2	39.03	6	Dodge Van	1971
Behr	Steve +	3	37.16	1	Cadillac Coupe De Ville	1972
Behr	Steve	4	38.03	3	Dodge Challenger	1975
Behr	Steve	5	42.27	28	Porsche 928	1979
Bell	Roger	5	58.04	39	Rolls-Royce Silver Wraith	1979
Bernius	Terry	5	44.13	32	Lotus Esprit	1979
Blue	Doug	3	49.04	25	Chevrolet Monte Carlo	1972
Brennan	Peter	5	0.00	45	Pontiac Firebird Trans Am	1979
Brio	Roman +	3	37.16	1	Cadillac Coupe De Ville	1972
Brock	Pete	3	37.33	3	Mercedes-Benz 280 SEL	1972
Brodrick	Bill	2	57.25	7	Travco Motorhome	1971
Brodrick	Bill	3	44.42	19	Travco Motorhome	1972
Brodrick	Bill	4	45.36	17	Travco Motorhome	1975
Brown	Bob	3	37.26	2	Dodge Challenger	1972
Brownell	Dave	5	61.51	40	Ford Panel Truck	1979
Browning	Bob	5	40.33	24	Volvo 242 GT	1979
Bruerton	Ed	2	37.48	5	AMC AMX	1971

Table 1 – continued

Last name	First name	Run	Time	Place	Vehicle	Year
Bruerton	Ed	3	39.42	8	AMC AMX	1972
Bruerton	Tom	2	37.48	5	AMC AMX	1971
Bruerton	Tom	3	39.42	8	AMC AMX	1972
Buffum	John	4	40.19	9	Porsche Carrera	1975
Buffum	Vicki	4	40.19	9	Porsche Carrera	1975
Cady	Jack	3	43.02	16	Ford Van	1972
Campbell	Bill	5	41.00	26	Ford Thunderbird	1979
Canfield	Bill +	3	37.16	1	Cadillac Coupe De Ville	1972
Cannata	Richard	4	44.23	16	Studebaker	1975
Carey	Bob	2	57.25	7	Travco Motorhome	1971
Carlson	Tim	4	40.37	11	Ford Van	1975
Catalano	Christine	5	35.17	6	Mazda RX-7	1979
Chapin	Kim	2	39.03	6	Dodge Van	1971
Cline	Rick +	4	35.53	1	Ferrari Dino 246 GTS	1975
Cooper	Bill	5	38.52	18	Ferrari 308 GT 350	1979
Corrizzoni	Tom	3	49.04	25	Chevrolet Monte Carlo	1972
Coumo	?	3	0.00	33	Studebaker	1972
Cowell	Jack	3	37.33	3	Mercedes-Benz 280 SEL	1972
Crabbe	Paul	3	45.39	21	Opel Rallye	1972
Cripe	Tom	5	44.13	32	Lotus Esprit	1979
Crittenden	Jim	5	36.00	8	Buick Park Avenue	1979
Dainko	Rainec	3	40.55	10	Chevrolet Van	1972
Davidson	Stuart	5	46.48	36	Ferrari 330 GT	1979
Dawn	Wes	2	0.00	8	MGB GT	1971
Dawn	Wes	3	39.35	7	Chevrolet Vega	1972
Dawn	Wes	4	38.16	4	Mercedes-Benz 450 SL	1975
Dawn	Wes	5	36.49	12	Cadillac Eldorado	1979
De Van	Fred	3	39.29	6	Mazda RX-2	1972
Defty	Peter	5	45.32	33	Chevrolet Suburban	1979
Denner	Tom	3	41.06	12	Chevrolet Vega	1972
Dennison	Scott	3	40.55	10	Chevrolet Van	1972
Doherty	Richard	5	35.17	6	Mazda RX-7	1979
Dornsife	Rod	5	42.27	28	Porsche 928	1979
Dunaj	Jon	5	36.19	9	Mercedes-Benz 300 D	1979
Durst	Steve	3	0.00	27	Chevrolet Vega	1972
Egloff	George	5	43.32	30	Suzuki 850 Motorcycle	1979
Ehrich	Terry	5	61.51	40	Ford Panel Truck	1979
Epstein	Wendy	5	43.32	30	Suzuki 850 Motorcycle	1979

Table 1 – continued

Last name	First name	Run	Time	Place	Vehicle	Year
Erickson	Morris	3	46.17	22	Opel Rallye	1972
Fassler	Paul	5	37.25	14	Porsche 930	1979
Faust	David	5	36.51	13	Chevrolet Malibu	1979
Feiner	Fred	3	0.00	33	Studebaker	1972
Feiner	Fred	4	44.23	16	Studebaker	1975
Fergusson	Alice	3	42.08	15	Citroën DS 19	1972
Fergusson	Joe	3	42.08	15	Citroën DS 19	1972
Fernald	Steve	4	40.31	10	Volvo 164 E	1975
Field	Dick	5	32.59	2	Mercedes-Benz 450 SEL 6.9	1979
Fischer	Paul	3	41.01	11	Ford Torino	1972
Fischer	Paul	4	40.53	13	Ford Torino	1975
Fog	Steven	5	34.07	4	Pontiac Firebird Trans Am	1979
Frankl	Andrew	5	65.55	41	Ford Mini Truck	1979
Fransson	Joe	3	44.42	19	Travco Motorhome	1972
Fuchs	John	3	41.15	13	American Hornet	1972
Gafford	Tom	5	45.32	33	Chevrolet Suburban	1979
Gallagher	?	3	0.00	34	Honda 600	1972
Garbarini	Steve	3	48.25	24	Datsun 240 Z	1972
Garcione	William	3	48.25	24	Datsun 240 Z	1972
Gilmartin	Richard	3	37.33	3	Mercedes-Benz 280 SEL	1972
Goodman	Kirby	5	36.51	13	Chevrolet Malibu	1979
Gould	Richard	4	41.35	15	Oldsmobile Cutlass	1975
Graham	Paul	5	39.45	22	Chevrolet Camaro	1979
Gregory	Fred	5	0.00	45	Pontiac Firebird Trans Am	1979
Gurney	Dan +	2	35.54	1	Ferrari Daytona	1971
Hammil	?	3	0.00	29	Porsche 911	1972
Harmston	Edwin	5	58.04	39	Rolls-Royce Silver Wraith	1979
Harris	Richard	3	0.00	33	Studebaker	1972
Harris	Richard	4	44.23	16	Studebaker	1975
Harrison	John	5	0.00	44	Lotus Esprit	1979
Heinz	Dave +	5	32.51	1	Jaguar XJS	1979
Henry	Bill	3	41.06	12	Chevrolet Vega	1972
Herisko	Ron	2	36.56	3	Cadillac Coupe De Ville	1971
Hickey	Tom	5	32.59	2	Mercedes-Benz 450 SEL 6.9	1979
Hitchins	John	5	65.55	41	Ford Mini Truck	1979
Honegger	Pierre	4	39.22	8	Mazda RX-4	1975
Hopkins	Danny	3	38.02	4	De Tomaso Pantera	1972
Hopkins	Hoppy	3	38.02	4	De Tomaso Pantera	1972

Table 1 – continued

Last name	First name	Run	Time	Place	Vehicle	Year
Hoschek	Gero	5	43.47	31	Jensen Interceptor	1979
Houge	Larry	3	46.17	22	Opel Rallye	1972
Hourihan	Bob	4	40.31	10	Volvo 164 E	1975
Howlett	Jack	4	38.45	6	Buick Electra	1975
Hunt	Jim	5	41.00	26	Ford Thunderbird	1979
James	Dirk	5	43.32	30	Suzuki 850 Motorcycle	1979
Jeanes	William	4	45.36	17	Travco Motorhome	1975
Jellison	Rich	3	57.19	26	Chevrolet Corvette	1972
Jenkins	Richard	3	38.37	5	Alfa Romeo Guilia	1972
Jessen	John	3	57.19	26	Chevrolet Corvette	1972
Jessick	Peter	5	40.53	25	Chrysler	1979
Johnson	Don	3	0.00	31	Austin Healey	1972
Johnson	Gary	4	37.50	2	Chevrolet Pickup	1975
Jones	David	5	38.10	17	Chevrolet Blazer	1979
Kendall-Lane	Fiona	5	58.04	39	Rolls-Royce Silver Wraith	1979
Kendall-Lane	Stephen	5	58.04	39	Rolls-Royce Silver Wraith	1979
Kenny	?	3	0.00	32	Chevrolet Camaro Z 28	1972
Kepler	Fred	3	0.00	32	Chevrolet Camaro Z 28	1972
Key	Robert	5	48.53	37	Shelby Mustang GT 350	1979
Kirby	Jim	5	36.40	11	Chevrolet Camaro Z 28	1979
Kopec	Rich	5	48.53	37	Shelby Mustang GT 350	1979
Kovaleski	Oscar	2	36.47	2	Chevrolet Van	1971
Kovaleski	Bob	4	36.40	11	Chevrolet Camaro Z 28	1979
Kozlowski	Tom	4	39.22	8	Mazda RX-4	1975
Lane	John	5	37.31	15	Porsche 928	1979
Leib	Dick	3	44.54	20	Pontiac	1972
Leonard	Tom	5	37.46	16	Chevrolet Camaro Z 28	1979
Lincoln	Sam	3	49.04	25	Chevrolet Monte Carlo	1972
Lloyd	David	5	36.00	8	Buick Park Avenue	1979
Locke	Pete	3	40.11	9	Chrysler	1972
Loveli	Bill	5	41.00	26	Ford Thunderbird	1979
Lynch	Leo	3	0.00	30	Porsche 911	1972
Lynch	Leo	4	38.39	5	Porsche 911	1975
Mahler	John	5	37.46	16	Chevrolet Camaro Z 28	1979
Marbut	Tom	2	37.45	4	Dodge Van	1971
Marget	Pete	3	41.41	14	Datsun 510	1972
Marshall	Pierce	5	36.51	13	Chevrolet Malibu	1979
Martin	Charles	5	45.32	33	Chevrolet Suburban	1979

Table 1 – continued

Last name	First name	Run	Time	Place	Vehicle	Year
Martin	Chauncey	3	43.02	16	Ford Van	1972
Martini	Jeff	4	39.22	8	Mazda RX-4	1975
Martini	Jeff	5	36.49	12	Cadillac Eldorado	1979
May	Jack +	4	35.53	1	Ferrari Dino 246 GTS	1975
Mayo	Edward	5	38.10	17	Chevrolet Blazer	1979
McCathey	Charlie	5	36.19	9	Mercedes-Benz 300 D	1979
McConkey	Ron	4	40.43	12	Pontiac Firebird Trans Am	1975
McCoy	Jack	4	37.50	2	Chevrolet Pickup	1975
McCoy	Peggy	4	37.50	2	Chevrolet Pickup	1975
McPaul	?	3	0.00	29	Porsche 911	1972
McGovern	John	4	41.35	15	Oldsmobile Cutlass	1975
McGovern	John	5	58.04	39	Rolls-Royce Silver Wraith	1979
McGrail	Tom	3	44.42	19	Travco Motorhome	1972
McGrail	Tom	4	45.36	17	Travco Motorhome	1975
McMeekan	George	3	44.54	20	Pontiac	1972
McPherson	Glen	3	0.00	31	Austin Healey	1972
McWhorter	Donald	5	41.17	27	Chevrolet Corvette	1979
McWhorter	Gerald	5	41.17	27	Chevrolet Corvette	1979
Menesini	Dennis	5	34.52	5	Chevrolet Pickup	1979
Menke	Vern	4	40.53	13	Ford Torino	1975
Menzel	Mike	5	0.00	46	Fiat 127	1979
Micek	John	5	40.53	25	Chrysler	1979
Miller	James	3	43.45	18	Bradley GT	1972
Miller	Mark	5	34.52	5	Chevrolet Pickup	1979
Miller	Robin	3	39.35	7	Chevrolet Vega	1972
Mims	Donna Mae	3	0.00	28	Cadillac Limousine	1972
Mockett	Doug	5	40.53	25	Chrysler	1979
Moody	Dave	3	41.01	11	Ford Torino	1972
Moore	Bill	5	40.53	25	Chrysler	1979
Morin	Holly	2	39.03	6	Dodge Van	1971
Morton	Tom	3	41.01	11	Ford Torino	1972
Morton	Tom	4	40.33	13	Ford Torino	1975
Moses	Sam	5	39.29	21	Ford Mustang Boss 302	1979
Mullen	Jim	5	40.11	23	Ferrari SWB	1979
Mullen	Joan	5	40.11	23	Ferrari SWB	1979
Needham	Hal	5	90.00	43	Dodge Van	1979
Nehl	Tom	4	41.32	14	Porsche 911	1975
Nerger	Ursula	5	43.47	31	Jensen Interceptor	1979

Table 1 – continued

Last name	First name	Run	Time	Place	Vehicle	Year
Nichols	John	5	39.45	22	Chevrolet Camaro	1979
Nickel	Gil	4	38.16	4	Mercedes-Benz 450 SL	1975
Niemcek	Brad	2	36.47	2	Chevrolet Van	1971
Niemcek	Brad	3	90.00	27	Chevrolet Van	1972
Niemcek	Brad	4	40.37	11	Ford Van	1975
Niemcek	Peggi	3	90.00	28	Cadillac Limousine	1972
Nunn	Spike	3	41.41	14	Datsun 510	1972
O'Brien	Robert	4	41.35	15	Oldsmobile Cutlass	1975
O'Donnell	Bill	5	53.00	38	Cadillac Eldorado	1979
Olds	Fred +	3	37.16	1	Cadillac Coupe De Ville	1972
Olds	Fred	4	40.31	10	Volvo 164 E	1975
Opert	Larry	2	36.56	3	Cadillac Sedan De Ville	1971
Poggio	Massimo	5	90.00	46	Fiat 127	1979
Parker	Pal	2	57.25	7	Travco Motorhome	1971
Parker	Pal	3	44.42	19	Travco Motorhome	1972
Parker	Pal	4	45.36	17	Travco Motorhome	1975
Pash	Phil	2	57.25	7	Travco Motorhome	1971
Patchett	Keith	5	72.54	42	BMW R 90/6 Motorcycle	1979
Pearson	Jack	4	38.45	6	Buick Electra	1975
Peeler	Jim	5	46.48	36	Ferrari 330 GT	1979
Perlow	Bob	2	90.00	8	MGB GT	1971
Pfeifer	S.	3	47.28	23	Ford Pinto	1972
Pierce	Jeff	5	33.42	3	Pontiac Firebird Trans Am	1979
Pitt	Jesse	3	40.11	9	Chrysler	1972
Poston	Becky	2	37.45	4	Dodge Van	1971
Prentiss	Larry	5	46.37	35	Porsche Carrera	1979
Pritch	Mark	5	36.52	18	Ferrari 308 GT 350	1979
Pritzker	Nate	2	36.56	3	Cadillac Sedan De Ville	1971
Pryor	Bill	4	49.32	18	Bristol 410	1975
Pryor	Bill	5	40.33	24	Volvo 242 GT	1979
Quartararo	Tony	5	46.48	36	Ferrari 330 GT	1979
Race	Donald	5	53.00	38	Cadillac Eldorado	1979
Ralston	Benjamin	5	46.37	35	Porsche Carrera	1979
Ramsey	John	3	43.28	17	Ford Torino	1972
Rasmussen	Buzz	5	39.20	20	Chevrolet El Camino	1979
Regan	Ken	4	40.37	11	Ford Van	1975
Richardson	Tad	5	35.17	6	Mazda RX-7	1979
Riggs	Clyde	5	36.49	12	Cadillac Eldorado	1979

Table 1 – continued

Last name	First name	Run	Time	Place	Vehicle	Year
Robison	Charlie	5	34.52	5	Chevrolet Pickup	1979
Roder	Dick	3	40.55	10	Chevrolet Van	1972
Romine	Chris	5	35.58	7	Ferrari 308 GTS	1979
Rosenblatt	Joel	5	36.00	8	Buick Park Avenue	1979
Rost	Bob	3	38.37	5	Alfa Romeo Guilia	1972
Rowzie	Dan	4	38.39	5	Porsche 911 RSR	1975
Royer	Lyle	5	90.00	43	Dodge Van	1979
Satullo	Sandy	4	38.45	6	Buick Electra	1975
Satullo	Sandy	5	36.49	12	Pontiac	1979
Satullo	Stuart	5	36.49	12	Pontiac	1979
Satullo II	Sandy	4	38.45	6	Buick Electra	1975
Satullo II	Sandy	5	36.49	12	Pontiac	1979
Scarlato	Jerry	4	45.36	17	Travco Motorhome	1975
Schmitt	Charles	5	53.00	38	Cadillac Eldorado	1979
Scott	Dick	3	90.00	30	Porsche 911	1972
Scribner	Doug	3	49.04	25	Chevrolet Monte Carlo	1972
Sellyei	Louis	5	39.10	19	Jaguar XJS	1979
Sencenbaugh	Jim	5	45.32	33	Chevrolet Suburban	1979
Seneki	Alex	5	46.31	34	Mercedes-Benz 300 SEL 6.3	1979
Shugars	Dave	4	40.43	12	Pontiac Firebird Trans Am	1975
Sibio	Albert Jr.	5	36.40	11	Chevrolet Camaro Z 28	1979
Simkin	Daniel	5	36.20	10	Excalibur	1979
Smith	Gary	5	39.45	22	Chevrolet Camaro	1979
Smith	Ken	5	34.52	5	Chevrolet Pickup	1979
Smith	Steve +	1	40.51	1	Dodge Sportsman Van	1971
Snyder	Michael	5	33.42	3	Pontiac Firebird Trans Am	1979
Solski	Paul	3	39.29	6	Mazda RX-2	1972
Sportiche	Alain	5	46.31	34	Mercedes-Benz 300 SEL 6.3	1979
Spreadbury	Bill	3	47.28	23	Ford Pinto	1972
Stanner	Bud	3	37.26	2	Dodge Challenger	1972
Stanton	Chick	4	38.56	7	Porsche Carrera	1975
Stanton	Chick	5	42.28	29	Porsche Carrera	1979
Stephenson	?	3	90.00	34	Honda 600	1972
Stevens	David	5	36.20	10	Excalibur	1979
Stropus	Judy	3	90.00	28	Cadillac Limousine	1972
Taayjes	Bob	3	43.45	18	Bradley GT	1972
Talbert	R.A.	3	44.54	20	Pontiac	1972
Taylor	Justus	5	61.51	40	Ford Panel Truck	1979

Table 1 – continued

Last name	First name	Run	Time	Place	Vehicle	Year
Thibeau	John	3	45.39	21	Opel Rallye	1972
Trefethen	Jon	3	43.28	17	Ford Torino	1972
Truesdale	Loyal	5	72.54	42	BMW R 90/6 Motorcycle	1979
Turkovich	Bob	4	40.37	11	Ford Van	1975
Unkefer	Duane	3	43.02	16	Ford Van	1972
Villeneuve	Jacques	5	37.31	15	Porsche 928	1979
Visniewski	Scott	5	38.10	17	Chevrolet Blazer	1979
Walle	Ray	4	39.22	8	Mazda RX-4	1975
Ward	Ken	5	43.32	30	Suzuki 850 Motorcycle	1979
Ward	Steve	5	43.32	30	Suzuki 850 Motorcycle	1979
Warner	Bill	4	41.32	14	Porsche 911	1975
Waters	Randy	2	37.45	4	Dodge Van	1971
Weglarz	Dennis	4	40.43	12	Pontiac Firebird Trans Am	1975
Whiteside	Mark	5	34.07	4	Pontiac Firebird Trans Am	1979
Williams	Jim +	1	40.51	1	Dodge Sportsman Van	1971
Williams	Willie	5	38.10	17	Chevrolet Blazer	1979
Willig	George	5	39.29	21	Ford Mustang Boss 302	1979
Yarborough	Dave +	5	32.51	1	Jaguar XJS	1979
Yates	Brock +	1	40.51	1	Dodge Sportsman Van	1971
Yates	Brock +	2	35.54	1	Ferrari Daytona	1971
Yates	Brock	3	37.26	2	Dodge Challenger	1972
Yates	Brock	4	38.03	3	Dodge Challenger	1975
Yates	Brock	5	90.00	43	Dodge Van	1979
Yates	Brock, Jr.	1	40.51	1	Dodge Sportsman Van	1971
Yates	Pamela	5	90.00	43	Dodge Van	1979
Ziegel	Robert	5	37.25	14	Porsche 930	1979
Zoeltner	Andreas	5	43.47	31	Jensen Interceptor	1979

I will leave you to read and digest this list. What springs to mind immediately is the diverse range of vehicles that took part – how the hell did a Jensen Interceptor complete a 3,000 mile journey? Interestingly, even the slowest vehicle in the list above is still quicker than the modern-day runs as these have the benefit of luxury stop-overs.

Modern-day races are now gathering momentum and gaining notoriety with the level of interest growing bigger and bigger each year. Phase two probably began in 1999 with Maximillion Cooper, who started The Gumball 3000. This race is widely accepted as being the most flamboyant car race running. However, it is so far distanced from the original roots of car racing epitomised by the *Cannonball* films, that only the extremely wealthy and famous can compete. The next two acknowledged European car races are The Cannonball 8000, which went bankrupt in 2008, and The Cannonball Run Europe.

In 1999 a new age of racing began. Maximillion Cooper called upon his close and well-connected friends and acquaintances and 55 cars were mustered and collectively driven to Rimini in Italy and back again, enjoying great parties and adventures – so much so that the race was back on again the following year. Could it be bettered? Well actually yes, the year 2000 saw the cars drive the short distance from London to Stansted airport in Essex and then promptly flown to Spain where again, via great parties and adventures, the cars returned to the UK via Cannes and Hamburg. That year also saw the start of greater commercial interest with Top Trumps signing a deal to feature a Gumball 3000 trumps game. The race was also attracting celebrities, who in turn attracted more media attention which made celebrities out of some of the drivers. In 2002, The Gumball departed European shores and went to the home of The Cannonball, going from New York to Los Angeles with the lucky finishers having a 'ball' at Hugh Hefner's Playboy Mansion. The Gumball stayed in the USA the following year, travelling from San Francisco to Miami. That year saw the emergence of two characters who have found notoriety from the race: Richard Rawlings and Alex Roy, two drivers who have jousted over the record for the trans-America crossing. This particular race also had the distinction of a reported 242mph speed of a Koenigsegg. To date, the highest recorded speeding violation was in 1971 with a ticket issued for 165mph.

The rally switched back to Europe and Africa in 2004, starting in Paris and ending in Cannes. However, the cars went via Marrakech, and a book was written about this rally, I believe the only book written to date on the subject. For the past three years The Gumball has started in London, drawing huge crowds. For the start of the 2007 race hundreds of thousands of people gathered, completely blocking Pall Mall and Piccadilly in central London as the cars left on a Sunday afternoon. Two of the crowd consisted of my youngest son Tom and myself. I say this as I have to confess that when I was looking into these rallies I found myself on what I thought was The Gumball site. With great excitement I declared to both my sons, Joseph being the eldest, that we would go and see the start of The Gumball in Ashford, Kent. We duly arrived at the Ashford International Hotel early, as I was prepared for the crowds, to find a nearly empty car park. As the start time grew closer we were still one of only a few cars in the car park. The boys were now beginning to wonder what all the fuss was about and secretly so was I.

'Look, an Aston Martin!' I shouted hysterically in justification that we had driven almost 100 miles to see this event. The car pulled up and a suave racing driver of a man got out. 'This is it!' Still in a state of hysteria. 'These Gumball rallies are clocked in secret!' I said. The boys looked up from their Gameboys and promptly looked down again. More cars slowly turned up, but their calibre wasn't what I had imagined. Without being able to contain myself any more, as by this time the crowd had swelled to a couple of kids on their BMXs, I decided to leave the sanctuary of my car, a Range Rover Sport, which certainly could have competed against the cars arriving, and head off into the hotel. A wedding show was in full swing and at the desk in the foyer sat a marshal, 'a Euro Enduro marshal'.

'Hi,' he said, 'have you entered the Range Rover?'

'No, I'm a prat that has driven almost 100 miles to see The Gumball,' I could have said, but I didn't. In fact I replied, 'No I'm thinking about doing it next year and as I live round the corner I thought I would pop along to see what it's like.' I never went back.

The past three rallies have been the ones that took Gumball 3000 to new heights. The 2006 event encompassed three continents with the cars travelling from London to Belgrade, then being flown to Phuket in Thailand and then travelling overland to Bangkok. From there they were flown to Salt Lake City where again it was overland to Los Angeles and the Playboy Mansion. This race was probably one of the highest points in Gumball history. Unfortunately, it was replaced the following year by its lowest point, the death of a local who was in collision with one of the participants. This caused the race to be cancelled. The tenth Gumball in 2008 returned to the USA, starting in San Francisco with the cars again being airlifted to China and finishing in Beijing to culminate with the Olympics. The competitors had a stop-over in North Korea, which begs the question as to whether this is a road race or a glorified holiday fly drive. The 2009 Gumball went back to its roots with a drive from Los Angeles to Miami, 100 per cent by road, via Vegas, Santa Fe, Dallas and New Orleans. An assortment of the super cars took part with two Bugatti Veyrons, a couple of Mercedes Mclarens, and the obligatory Porsches and Mercedes. 2010 actually sees the return to London of the Gumball, where it starts, and finishing in New York via Scandinavia and Canada.

Cannonball 8000 and The Cannonball Run seemed still to retain the essence of the road race while still having fun. Started in 2003 by Conrad Wall, Cannonball 8000 was a much shorter event spanning a long weekend and was solely raced over Europe. Again, as the years rumbled by, so the profile of this event grew, with it being televised on terrestrial and digital television in recent years. In 2009 it planned to compete in the Far East. In 2008, its last run, saw it organise a very wet Manchester to Brighton run before going into a mysterious bankruptcy.

So to The Cannonball Run Europe, which was started in 2002 by Tim Porter, and has recently been taken over by Jan Dechamps. This rally spans both Europe and the USA with an event in both countries. The US rally is known as The Great American Run, this making it the closest one to the original Cannonball. The European Cannonball takes place over six days and travels almost 3,000 miles. What's it like? Read on and all will be revealed. However, a taster of what's to come sums this particular rally up: keeping to its roots. In one particular country it passed through, this time, the drivers were rounded up by the police and asked in no uncertain terms to leave the country for 'illegal road racing' – now that's Cannonball!

More recent events have now outlived the original and outgrown it as well. The raw excitement of the races in the 1970s must have been spectacular. Certainly the modern drivers get their own buzz, their own excitement, but more importantly they are doing the runs, on the whole, technology wise, in cars that are light years ahead of the cars that took part 30-odd years ago. They are doing the runs with television and film crews following them, perhaps scripting them in places! They are arriving in towns and cities and meeting dignitaries and in some cases, heads of state and royalty. The whole thing has moved on leaps and bounds; however, what remains is the camaraderie of the participants, and while there are all the attractions and the hangers-on 'the sheer hell of it' is still the overriding factor that consumes most of the drivers. To say you have participated in one of these races leaves you feeling ten feet tall.

5

Smart Car: the Beginnings

In the beginning in a land far, far, away lived a man called Otto. Nicolaus August Otto to be precise, and he lived a long time ago. Who can remember 1976? The first commercial flight of Concorde, a year in which the Queen sent her first email, yes that's right an email sent in 1976, and Apple computers were formed. No? Still hazy? A year in which the Brazilian footballer Ronaldo and Emma Bunton of the Spice Girls were born and the Brotherhood of Man won the Eurovision Song Contest with 'Save All Your Kisses For Me'. Sid James died and Nikki Lauder was seriously burnt in the German Grand Prix. Coming back to you now? Well, this should give it to you. Jimmy Carter became President of the United States and if you're still struggling then The Sex Pistols met Bill Grundy!

Otto wouldn't have known anything about those events but he, 100 years earlier, in 1876, invented the gas engine. Not content with that he progressed onto the first four-stroke internal combustion engine which he placed into a motorcycle. He came up with the name the 'Otto Cycle Engine'. Rather pleased with himself, no doubt, he sat back, a dangerous thing to do in the early engine design wars of the late nineteenth century, as nine years later Gottlieb Daimler then laid claim to inventing the gas engine which became generally recognised as the main forerunner of the modern gas engine. This engine also opened the avenue to car design, leading to the first car to be built from ground up in 1889 by Daimler Maybach. While the Daimler Maybach/Otto scrap was going on, another force was awakening in Germany, namely Karl Freidrich Benz, who in 1885 designed and built the first automobile powered by an internal combustion engine. A year later in 1886 he received a patent for the first fuel-powered automobile. This was built as a three-wheeler car but in 1891 Benz started building four-wheel cars and the rest, as they say, is history.

Now why would I go on about the history of the automobile when we are discussing the Smart car? Well, it hopefully hasn't escaped your attention that the names mentioned previously play a big part in the Smart car: Daimler and Benz. So if anyone asks when the Smart car was conceived you could be really 'smart' and say the late 1800s.

Coming up to date, and the emergence of the Smart car, the story starts in 1993 with the Eco Speedster and Eco Sprinter which were, in 1994, lost to the current style we now see – the 'Fortwo', and as this is the car I competed in I will concentrate on this style of Smart. Contrary to what you might think, the Smart car was not invented by Mr Smart – that accolade, in fact, goes to a Nicolas Hayek, a Lebanese national who was the CEO of the Swatch group, which primarily made watches with interchangeable faces which were extremely popular. He is accredited with almost single-handedly turning round the fortunes of the Swatch group and turning it into the force it is today. Not content with turning round Swatch and the Swiss watch industry, Hayek diverted some of his attention to cars and came up with the concept of the Smart car. Unlike most of us who have doodled a car on a piece of paper, he took his doodle further and contacted Volkswagen and showed them his designs. For one reason or another Volkswagen decided not to see the concept through (similarly Ferrari never got back to me with my stunning four-door diesel estate design I sent them) but undeterred, Hayek approached Daimler-Benz who obviously saw a market for his car. As an inspirational point to all us car-doodlers, Nicolas Hayek in 2007 was 80 years old and was ranked in the world's richest 300 men, with an approximate wealth of $3.2 billion.

'Smart' means 'Swatch Mercedes Art'. The logo found on the cars denotes a C for compact and an arrow for forward-thinking. Smart is also technically spelt without a capital, though for the purpose of this book we have used one for the sake of aesthetics. This forward thinking actually 'lost' Hayek because the final design didn't live up to his expectations, primarily due to the Smart having a conventional engine rather than a hybrid or electrical one, as favoured by Hayek. In the advent of time and justifying Hayek's 'forward thinking', in 2008 an electrically powered Smart Fourtwo was presented and utilised by a Midlands based city council. 'Smart' also refers to 'opening your mind', a concept much vaunted in the promotional material for the car.

The production of the car subsequently proved far too expensive, leading to Hayek and Swatch pulling out of the partnership. Before this happened, Swatch and Daimler-Benz had constructed a purpose-built factory called Smartville at Hambach in Lorraine, France, where the cars are now produced. Interestingly, the region of Lorraine is the only one out of France's 26 regions that borders three countries: Belgium, Luxemburg and Germany, and coupled with the Rhine, Moselle, Meurthe and the Meuse rivers flowing through it, the region has taken an important role in European affairs whilst still having time to produce over 1,000,000 Smart cars.

The Smart hit the European audience in 1997 in Frankfurt, Germany. The car, by all accounts, was met with a positive response and was subsequently launched in nine European countries a year later, with the first one rolling off the production line in July 1998, ten years before one roared off The Cannonball start line in 2008. Its unique appearance soon made an impact on the European motor industry and on the streets of Europe. Its size, at only 8.5ft long, less than 5ft wide and 5ft tall, meant that it drew huge attention to itself as it buzzed round Europe's capitals. The general specification figures given for these cars consisted of both the 50- and 61-hp engines which are three cylinder models, with cooled turbochargers. According to Smart, the 61hp engine can go from 0 to 60mph in about 15 seconds, while the top speed is electronically limited to 84mph for the driver's safety. You will read later how we threw caution to the wind and lived extremely dangerously by topping in excess of 120mph but, hey, 'that's Cannonball'. In city driving, the Fortwo gets a reported 46.3mpg, while on the highway it delivers an even more impressive 68.9mpg. We got 35, but hey that's still Cannonball. The 50hp engine accelerates more slowly, but the electronic speed limit is the same, and the mpg ratings are the same.

The Smart's appearance has been described as a 'box on wheels' with the front cut down; however, this actually belies its stability level and the 'high length to width ratio' certainly helps its cornering ability. It is also one of the lightest four-wheel vehicles currently on European roads, theoretically making it very unsafe in a collision. Not so: to combat this and make the car as safe as possible, Smart constructed the car utilising a Tridion steel safety shell. This is a steel cage which encloses the interior of the car while forming the bulk of the car's chassis. There is an energy-absorbing zone at the front of the car and of course the engine can be found at the rear. The steel shell also adds something to the look of the car as it shows through from the outside.

The remainder of the car takes the original design from Hayek's original plan, with the interchangeable panels which allow the owner to change the colour by just replacing them, similar, obviously, to Swatch watches. Aesthetically, this is pleasing to any owner who can change the appearance of their car on a weekly basis if they so wish. It is also beneficial should the car be in an accident and in the event of any damage – body panels can be simply replaced, therefore making the process of repairs a lot quicker and more economic. As I previously mentioned, I have limited this information to the Fortwo, however Smart have also produced other versions including the 'Forfour', 'Roadster', 'Crossblade' and 'Formore'. Presently only the Fortwo is in production, the other models having been discontinued. If you'd like to know more about Smarts, I recommend the book *Smart Thinking* by Tony Lewin. If you would like more detailed information on The Cannonball Run there is a great book called *Cannonball* written by the man himself, Brock Yates.

So the quirky little car you see zipping round the roads has now had a revamp, in 2008: only a little revamp, just enough for the untrained eye to notice that it is now slightly longer, with slightly different body panels and is becoming known as the '451'.

The new brochure offers an insight into the real quirkiness of the car. For example, it questions: 'Why does a car need a rear seat when it only carries one or two people?' 'Isn't a bonnet a waste of space when the engine can go in the rear?' 'Why is a clutch pedal needed when automatic driving is best suited to town?' The new Smart comes in four variations. The 'Pure' is the basic model, designed for those seeking functionality and economy. The 'Pulse' is a Pure but with a bit more get up and go, coupled with alloy wheels, and a sporty-looking rev counter and clock, and is currently putting out 71hp. The 'Passion' was my first model and offers a few more refinements such as electric windows, electric door mirrors, air conditioning and more substantial choices of interior finishes. Then we come to the 'Brabus'

The joint venture between Smart and Brabus created the Smart 'Gmbh'. The difference between this car and the other Smart models is extremely noticeable. As soon as you get into the car it feels more solid, sturdier and bigger than its counterparts. The interior comes in leather, complete with leather steering wheel and shift paddles. The pedals and handbrake are finished in stainless steel and matt aluminium respectively. The seats are all round much better and come with heating. The car also has side airbags. Outside we have Monoblock V1 alloy wheels, front spoiler with larger air intakes, and a Brabus sports exhaust that pokes out of the middle of the back of the car. Allowing it to prowl the streets is the Brabus sports suspension which makes the car shout its intension to be fast. Finally, the one thing it has that no other Smart has is: the speedometer reads 120mph.

6

So Let the Carnival Begin

The idea of sponsorship hit me when following a car with a NCK spark plug sticker on it. I don't know what drew my attention to it (the power of advertising probably had something to do with it and I probably should have stuck it on the front of this book!), and smarts r us had said that they would do something nearer the event when I bought the car from them; so armed with this I decided to get my creative juices going and in a lull at work I began to put some ideas down.

I got the car cleaned by 'Hey Guys', a group of eastern European car cleaners who operate near where I live. I call them that as when they get a tip a chorus of 'hey guys' rings out and this keeps me amused and also costs me a fortune in car cleaning. Gleaming (when is it not) and driving past a derelict building I decided to stop and take some photos of the car. I liked one showing the back wheel arch and petrol cap and this became the backdrop to the idea of a postcard-type of leaflet which I could send out. On the computer I managed to arrange for the text I prepared to be imposed onto the photo and to celebrate this fantastic bit of computer wizardry I opened a bottle of white, closely followed by another.

Two days later I found my picture, text still imposed on it, cleverly saved under something so totally remote from the actual thing it should have been. My idea then was to print off say 20 or 30 of these, but my computer knowledge was found lacking and I couldn't do it, so a good old-fashioned printer was needed. I found one and decided to go for it: 500 were printed – it could have been

1,000 but common sense prevailed and in any case I was of the belief the professionalism of the postcard would do the job and it wouldn't be long before Coca-Cola, Virgin, *The Sun* newspaper, and numerous others would all be vying for my car.

The MPH show was at Earls Court in November with Jeremy Clarkson, and the other two. The gods were smiling on me! All I had to do was to take the postcards and hand them out, chat to Jeremy, Richard and James, and they would be mightily impressed with the plan. Failing that, if I was too busy to catch their attention, the postcards could be dispersed generally and 'bingo', the calls would come flooding in, the highest bidders found, contracts signed and Bob's your uncle the car is all sponsored. Wipe the brow, another job done.

The show was very good – I went with my boys, and they were dispatched to exhibitors to hand out said postcards. I networked at the bar and the girl serving was at first generally interested in the concept of a Smart car competing with the finest cars driving across Europe, although she did ask if I knew any of the drivers driving any of the finest cars quite often, and in between serving other customers asked a few pertinent questions. 'Like another?' was the most pertinent and 'Yes' my most common answer. The boys returned, not out of cards, and I sent them off again as I felt sure that the bar networking was going well, as now both girls (who looked alike) behind the bar did seem keen on sponsoring me. I would have taken a contribution from them, however they started not to take me seriously and speak some sort of gibberish while swaying around. Just as I was going to tell them what I thought of their stupid antics and enquire as to where the twin had come from my boys returned, postcard-less and off we went. Thinking back, the MPH show was indoor and therefore very hot, causing me to sweat profusely and the obvious dehydration caused me to walk fairly uneasily and completely forget my journey home. Added to that I was sick with a terrible headache the next morning.

Taking stock the next day, all 120 cards has been distributed and now, let the phone ring or the emails ping . . .

Having checked the postcard countless times – yes the phone number and email were correct, I quickly became resigned to the fact that the recession had obviously kicked in and that was why no one had responded. Phase 2 of the sponsorship plan now had to be brought in. Having sat down and scoured the internet, various magazines and what was left of my grey matter, I came up with a list of people who would benefit from being plastered across a Smart car as it hurtled across Europe, racing against Ferraris, Bentleys, Porsches, Audis, etc.

A card was sent to each with a hope and prayer from me that they would respond and the calls would come flooding in. Within days Pepsi emailed me to say they would not be interested as my proposal didn't fit their criteria. I was undeterred as I still had 92 desperate sponsors out there, and with smarts r us already showing signs of sponsorship the rest would follow.

I can only presume, having checked again that the cards had the right phone number and email address on them, which they did, that the recession was now really kicking in or that East London had a lightning post strike on the same day that all 94 cards were posted.

I now was having a 'warm down' on the sponsorship idea and comforted myself in the knowledge that all the people who totally ignored my request for sponsorship would regret it when we won The Cannonball and appeared on all the top daytime TV shows. *That will show them*, I laughed to myself, as I finished off a nice bottle of Chablis, only spoilt by the Tesco store detective asking if I would pay for it in, if I may add, a rather aggressive manner.

So the sponsorship idea was dead and buried but I still had about 200 of the cards left and I supposed that with some glue and glitter the Christmas cards would be taken care of that year.

I contacted the NSPCC to request details of sponsorship and hit upon the idea of a £10 slip or £15 slip which would show your name or company name on the car, give you a direct link to our website plus you would be kept in touch with what is going on, on a monthly basis, all for £10 or £15 depending on how large you wanted your name on the car, therefore capitalising on the numerous double barrelled names of south west London. Armed with this new idea yes, you've guessed it, 'bingo', the calls would come flooding in.

So who would I target for this? My 35 acquaintances for a start, which would equate to £350 minimum – not really anything to shout about. Perhaps I could target all the football teams in the Premiership, Championship, First, Second and Scottish Premiership, in total 104 teams grossing millions every Saturday, Sunday and if on ESPN, Monday nights and Wednesday lunchtimes or something like that. All I wanted was £10, possibly £15, from each of them and of course them all being kind and generous people, away we would go. After painstakingly slogging through the clubs' websites, most of which were, surprisingly, the same, I found with the help of my good friend who had flown in from Bordeaux via the wine aisle at Tesco, a full list of email addresses. On Tuesday 27 November 2007 the new plan rolled into action and off went the emails, rather cleverly titled 'A McClaren team still doing something this summer', which was obviously a pun on the plight of Steve McClaren, the ex-England manager who managed to get England out of the 2008 European Championships, and McLaren Mercedes who were competing in the Grand Prix that year.

First to respond was Chelsea FC, who informed me that I should write to another department, and this I duly did. Second to respond was Liverpool FC, who said that they couldn't help. Nor could Celtic FC. Coming in fourth were Port Vale who again couldn't help, but Sharon there suggested I write to Lee Sinnett, the manager, with some items the players could autograph, which I did. I sent them two of the initial adverts for sponsors that everyone had totally ignored, for them to sign. I must have got the address wrong or written to the wrong Port Vale as I never heard back from them!

While all this was going on, and again sitting in my gleaming car I heard an advert on Heart FM, someone else who had totally blanked my sponsor request. Now you might suggest that I should have blanked them in return, but if I did that I wouldn't be listening to anything other than Radio 3 or 4, who I believe were the only radio stations I didn't write to. I heard an advert for a boat show at Earls Court from 1 to 7 December. My ears pricked up. Sunday 2nd would see the return of operation postcard distribution. Going back to the football clubs, West Brom responded with a 'No we can't help you' and I countered with a 'Can I send you a leaflet for signing by a few players anyway?' They came back saying yes but I needed to send them £5 for the privilege, which would go to their charity. To be honest when I thought about it I couldn't name a single player who played for them, and at roughly the same time found myself in the wine aisle in Tesco, where a greatly reduced bottle of Chablis at £4.99 screamed BUY ME! I bought the bottle and still had a penny change.

It must be said that I did show a certain naivety in thinking that I would receive a response from the clubs, as in retrospect an unsolicited email giving my address, telephone numbers and email could be seen as trying it on for £10. No other club even had the courtesy to either acknowledge or respond, even in the negative, except one. Milton Keynes Dons kindly sent me a voucher for two adults and two children to see a home game, for me to sell to raise funds. A gesture like that has gone a long way, and to them again a big thank you.

The football clubs are not the only ones. It would appear that the bigger the company the less 'people friendly' they are. I am certainly not advocating that all companies must give money to everyone who writes to them. Unfortunately there are a lot of scammers and con people out there, but it really does take a second just to respond, even to say no, and a no sometimes goes a long way, well not far really but you get the idea.

Sunday morning, 2 December came quickly and Earls Court beckoned. The night before I was only a mile or two away at Human League concert in Hammersmith, so that weekend was spent yo-yoing across London from my home to West London. The Earls Court arena had been the venue for the first failed advertising campaign at the MPH show, so heartened by the fact that there would be at least one or two hospitality stalls plus the show sponsors, Whyte & Mackay, I thought it would prove to be a good show with or without any boats. Arriving at 11.30 a.m. I was confronted by a near-empty arena which to be honest was a bit disconcerting. I wandered around for a while, having sent the boys off again to do their stuff. I in turn hovered around the hospitality venues only to find most of them empty with a couple of bored bar staff. This was proving to be a bit of a dilemma as I did not want to be the only one in a bar, this early. I decided the best course of action was to wander around the event, where I saw some boats, some boat accessories, some more accessories, some more boats and a lot of very keen salesmen and women who saw me approaching and then saw me go 'sailing' past them. I wandered upstairs, primarily to look down to see if I could spot my boys, and found myself at a section that had the bike and boat used by Jason Lewis in his epic 45,000-mile circumnavigation around the world. I stood in admiration at his feat of circumnavigating the globe in 13 years by self-propulsion and thought about the opposite end of the spectrum, with me trying to do 3,000 miles in the quickest time I could. His friend's father was at the stand and I spoke to him for a while, and it became abundantly clear that their appeals for sponsorship had been far from an easy task, and I was uplifted by my own efforts. After all, I was only looking for sponsorship for a week-long event, not 13 years! I was solely raising money for charity and not to fund 'my dream', so I threw caution to the wind. A two-pronged attack was needed: corporate sponsors on one side and mates and the general public on the other. I pulled the boys out of the 'heat of battle'; they had given out a few leaflets and bought a few boats, but were bored, so off home we went.

Tesco beckoned and I wandered round followed by an anxious-looking member of staff, or it could have been a flustered shopper, as it was only a couple of weeks to Christmas and Tesco, of course, had the temerity to shut for two days. My little mind game started: how long can I hold out before the wine and spirit aisle calls me?

Not long, as per normal, 'this gamey earthy Gigondas is worth the search', so said Jane Macquitty of *The Times* – that was a sign on the shelf, not the anxious looking person who I thought was following me. Well, that will do for me I thought – mind you it could have just said 'bottle of red wine'. Was it gamey and earthy? Who knows? I believe the cold lager before it could have impaired my appreciation of it. Never mind, my new plan was in place.

1   104 emails to the Premiership, Championship, First and Second Divisions plus the Scottish league.
2   Premiership (already sent).
3   104 emails to media and publications companies.
4   104 emails to estate agents and property companies.
5   104 emails to solicitors and accountants.
6   104 emails to the car industry (give them another chance).
7   Approaching friends' members of the public and fundraising.

7

The Year of The Cannonball

I arrived into 2008 via the Buddha Bar in Dubai and within the first three hours of the year couldn't actually tell anyone what year, time or date it was. Yes, my drink had obviously been spiked, but which drink could be hard to tell. The night was a grandiose black tie affair with guests arriving in all sorts of Ferraris, Lamborghinis Bentleys Rolls-Royces etc. and seemed to go on all night. My confusion really kicked in when at 4 a.m. my mobile started ringing and there were all sorts of people wishing me a Happy New Year and there I was in this incredibly spinning hotel room (they really have everything in Dubai). Was this going to be a forerunner for The Cannonball? Loads of drink, loads of well-heeled people, fantastic cars, and the mother of all parties? Perhaps this was a sign!

The next few days were then spent relaxing, reading and networking. I wasn't just there for partying and the sun, I was networking for zoomzoomsmart. This networking, as such, really consisted of me cornering one of the concierges at the hotel, amazingly one I had not made a fool of myself in front of in the early hours of the new year, and thrusting a book about The Gumball 3000 plus a few of my leaflets at them and then explaining that The Cannonball is similar, read my leaflet, and with all the people he meets every day, have a word, so to speak, and there's a few quid in it for him! He gratefully took the book and genuinely looked indebted to me for giving it to him. He took the leaflets and genuinely looked enthusiastic about them, and said that he would look forward to reading the book and would definitely speak to people about the leaflets! I left him, content that I had done as much as I could in Dubai to raise the image of the car, and decided to spend the next few days relaxing. It was on a trip to the Emirates Mall, a large shopping mall with a ski slope, that I saw one of those priceless moments that leaves you smiling even if you haven't been given any money or involves Millwall losing! The cars in Dubai are definitely something special and even at the shopping malls the cars in the car park would definitely outclass those in a Premiership football club's players' parking zone. While waiting for a taxi in probably the best taxi queue in the world, as you snake round the valet parking area which obviously attracts the crème de la crème of the cars, a car pulled up out of sight to the valet's but in ours. The driver got out and nonchalantly wandered up to a valet and tossed him the key, barking something in Arabic. 'It's the black one over there mate,' I think I heard him say, although my Arabic is not that good, I have to be honest. This valet, who couldn't have been over 20, started to wander over and as he got closer I could see him start to get slower and slower. He then looked at the keys and back at the car and then at the keys and again at the car, and then turned round with a smile that would match that of say Robbie Savage winning Professional Footballer of the Year. As I said my Arabic isn't perfect but I think he said, 'I'm 19 and that old bloke has just given me the keys to a fucking black Porsche Carrera GT.' Now I'm not sure at that point in time who was the cooler, the 19-year-old with the mouth of a sewer or the old guy who nonchalantly threw the keys at him. I decided it was the old guy.

I left the sun, cars, and 'lifestyle' of Dubai and returned to grey, drab London. It was 2008, the year of The Cannonball.

January offered three different exhibitions so I went back to what I know best: working the bars of the great exhibition halls.

January is the first month of the year in the Julian and Gregorian calendars and one of seven Gregorian months with the length of 31 days. January begins (astrologically) with the sun in the sign of Capricorn and ends in the sign of Aquarius. Astronomically speaking, the sun begins in the constellation of Sagittarius and ends in the constellation of Capricorn. January is named after Janus

(Ianuarius), the god of the doorway; the name has its beginnings in Roman mythology, where the Latin word for door (*ianua*) comes from. Therefore January is the door to the year. I bet you thought you had picked up the wrong book, didn't you!

My door having been thrust open at about 12.01 this year was by 5 January still ajar but hanging loosely from some rusty old screws and badly needing a new coat of varnish. Some injection of something was needed but I had no plan, no inclination and no idea. The contrast to the end of the previous year was startling. The website was now online but with no blog, yet, the car (the world beater) was sat outside my house looking forlorn, if a car can look like that, and the inclination to drive 12 miles to work was lacking let alone a 3,000-mile trip. West Ham got knocked out of the FA cup and of course the tax self-assessment had to be in by the end of the month. It was getting depressing, the uplifting buzz of the new venture before Christmas seemed light years away. I couldn't even raise the enthusiasm to visit my mates in the wine aisle at Tesco. Something had to give, as the shows were looming and I had to be at my cutting best. Talking about cutting, before the new year I had had my hair cut quite short for me and had the centre highlighted to facilitate the slightly eccentric look I wanted for the black tie affair on New Year's Eve. When The Cannonball started I would have orange and white flecks to match the car, as my plan was to have the car painted orange and white to maximise its appearance. Also, as my hair is thinning – when it does finally fall out it won't be down to age; I can blame all the stuff I put on it!

I needed a lift and as if by magic got it by way of an email. Going back to work I received a reply from a printer I had got in touch with ages ago. Having been ignored by so many people with my emails, even a response from someone I was going to give money to, as opposed to get money from, was a lift and this certainly sprung me into action.

With the great help of Louise Catterall of Trade Service Direct I created a T-shirt design which manifested itself on 100 shirts, 2,000 stickers and 5,000 leaflets. Still in a state of excitement about this, I pushed on and spoke to Tony and Matt at Image Worx in Harlow, who put my Union Jack design onto vinyl and more importantly onto my car, and I must say it exceeded my expectations and looked brilliant. My original idea of an orange and white design was dropped in favour of the Union Jack. I was on a roll now and the emails started again, my rapidly growing list ranging from Timmy Mallet, the children's entertainer of the 70s and 80s through to directors of Pepsi, via Marc Almond, the singer, and Linda Barker, the person! Were all in line for another visit along with a further 1,500 emails telling all and sundry about the T-shirt and how great the car looked. The car wasn't finished, however. I contacted Pentagon Glass who in the past have tinted the glass of a couple of my cars and they kindly arranged to do the Smart; again, the whole look of the car changed and it was really taking shape. People would stare and point at it and I was also now being asking questions about the Smart when I was at the petrol station or parked. The car definitely seemed to be catching people's imagination, which was good.

I spoke to smarts r us who again informed me that roadster wheels would be best suited to the car rather than the alloys I currently had, as the roadsters were more robust than the Brabus wheels and less inclined to buckle if hit at high speed. It was decided to go for the 15in alloys which would be sprayed black. This, I believed, was the penultimate piece of the jigsaw, the final piece being my old nemesis, the advertising. I had room for about seven adverts, two of which would be free and one of which was taken up by the 'Ticket to Ride Surf Company'. I also had two other companies now bubbling for adverts and obviously the Image Worx logos were going on. Early February would see the car finished except for the future corporate sponsorship. It's bizarre that from a very negative start at the beginning of January, in the space of a couple of weeks, the car had made a transition to leave it almost finished and ready for the rally, plus I had the merchandise and leaflets to really push on with the sponsorship. A visit to the 'Destinations' travel show also beckoned in early February plus the

Adventure travel show in late January.

Islington, and in particular Upper Street, has always been recognised for its trendy bars and fashionable eateries, and while I'm not the area's biggest fan, I always enjoy the occasional trip there, particularly a couple of bars that always seem to contain the local eccentrics or, even funnier, the wannabe-stars who could keep me amused for hours with their ludicrous attempts to be noticed by anyone and their outrageous tales of how they were in *London's Burning* and do I remember them as the neighbour of the old lady whose house burnt down when Glenn Murphy carried her out? 'Have you done much since?' I would invariably ask the wannabe. 'No!' was always the answer. All the wannabes' stories revolve around *Eastenders* and *London's Burning*, and a walk-on part. I think that over the past 15 years, half of Islington's pub population have had a walk-on part in these two iconic programmes.

London is rapidly changing and not necessarily for the best. Testament to this was the makeshift shrine to another stabbing victim outside the Angel Tube station which I had to pass to get to the Design and Business Centre to visit the Adventure travel show. Having witnessed the flowers and cards, which were looking forlorn and grubby mainly due to the rumbling traffic constantly passing by, this contrasted strongly with the show, with its upbeat, healthy-looking staff selling magical trips to all these far off destinations. Having the good fortune to be able to travel and enjoy such things I thought of the victim down the road: he would never enjoy the salt water of an ocean while surfing, or that initial blast of heat that revives us after a long flight as we get off the plane; the tingle of the first-night sunburn. Why? Because in general he was living his dream in a street gang who rarely strayed from their patch, and when he did just that, all he felt was a damp, cold pavement, if he was lucky. It's incidents like this that bring home the facts of life – you can choose two different paths, that are, in this case, merely 50 yards apart in Islington. It brings home the ideal that 'within reason go on and do it': with that motto life can be so different and exciting.

Bearing in mind the local area and its trendy bars, I was, and I think the only word for it was, devastated: the Business Design Centre had no bloody bar. I was forced, sober, and on my own, to visit the stands and talk to the exhibitors while pushing my own agenda of the Smart car and The Cannonball. I must say that talking, finally, to people who aren't in bars about my rally was quite interesting and I picked up some good vibes and some emails from companies to correspond with, leaving the exhibition with an upbeat feeling. I was now firmly back on track with the whole thing. It was time to crank the pressure up on both corporate and individual sponsors and with the car now taking shape and attracting attention the zoomzoomsmart circus was definitely 'rolling into town'.

January finished on a Thursday. I had one more day to wait for the T-shirts, stickers and leaflets, due on 1 February. The car was going to have the wheels fitted and two sponsors had now pledged sponsorship. January had been a productive month.

February is the second month of the year in the Julian and Gregorian calendars . It is the shortest month and the only month with fewer than 30 days. The month has 29 days in leap years, when the year number is divisible by four. February begins, astronomically speaking, with the sun in the constellation of Capricorn and ends with the sun in the constellation of Aquarius. Astrologically speaking, February begins with the sun in the sign of Aquarius and ends in the sign of Pisces.

The fruits of labour in January began to bear further fruit in February with the arrival of the T-shirts, stickers and leaflets. Another batch of 'flooding emails' was sent, keeping the name alive so to speak, and the leaflets were beginning their distribution. The sixth of the month marked the six months to go stage and with the able assistance of Mathew Dukes of the *Daily Mail* who kindly recommended a bottle of red containing a juicy berry fruit flavour plus alcohol, which helped, the countdown began in earnest. Just to clear a little matter up: Mathew Dukes isn't a mate or associate; he put his name to a bottle of red in the Tesco wine aisle which I found myself down while popping in to buy some Toilet Duck or something.

Theoretically I should have been arrested but I believe it is solely down to the consummate stupidity shown by those who describe themselves as 'technical people' who in their infinite wisdom tried to help with a computer glitch I was having and subsequently re-formatted everything on my computer! I, as you can imagine, was none too pleased and in a terse conversation with one of these monkeys threatened to do things which did constitute an assault. Buoyed by the good fortune of not having charges pressed by the prat who ruined my computer, I pushed on and picked up the phone but unfortunately, the high street computer company, well not high street, more industrial park, computer company took two weeks to repair my computer. I did manage to secure a further sponsor for the car so out of the bad came some good. The month was trickling by when I decided that not being content with T-shirts, leaflets and stickers most of which were still in the box, I would also commission 500 badges to go with them which I duly did and these were ordered.

The car was still courting a lot of attention when driving around Essex, Hertfordshire and London, and on a particular trip into London one Saturday I noticed that the website in subsequent days had a surge of hits and that was without giving out leaflets or any merchandise whatsoever. This obviously encouraged me and I was eagerly looking forward to March and the car show season and hopefully better weather which would bring more people out. Towards the end of February I wasn't really conscious of achieving a great deal. However I had managed to get the car up to 'smarts r us' and have the wheels swapped for a set of black-painted steels with Bridgestone tyres. The wheels now really set the car off and March beckoned. By the end of March the car would be finished and I could then concentrate on the fundraising for the NSPCC and hopefully give out some more of the 5,000 leaflets, 2,000 stickers, 500 badges and 100 T-shirts that I had become quite attached to and individually named.

8

Fan Mail

March is the third month of the year in the Gregorian calendar and one of seven months with a length of 31 days. The name comes from ancient Rome when March was the first month of the year and was called *Martius* after Mars, the Roman god of war. In Rome, where the climate is Mediterranean, March is the first month of spring, a logical point for the beginning of the year as well as the start of the military campaign season. March is also the month of the birthday of the soon to be acclaimed author David Ward.

The beginning of March found me roaming the streets. Well, it was my birthday and those all-day drinking fests were traditional, but no, I was roaming the streets of Chelsea, Kensington and Covent Garden in London, distributing leaflets and this, coupled with driving the car into London a few times, saw an increase in traffic on the website. It is always eye-opening wandering round London and if you are prepared to keep your eyes peeled there's always a celebrity to spot, and this occasion proved just so, I having spotted Steve Pemberton of *The League of Gentlemen* wandering through Chinatown. The leaflets were being left on all the Smarts I could find plus other cars whose owners I thought would appreciate The Cannonball Run.

I was called to Bishops Stortford in Hertfordshire to pay for a golfing holiday later in the year and was running late. I decided that in my haste I would use the time to test the car and practise 'The Gumball style of driving' even though I was doing The Cannonball Run. I was actually making good time when I came off a roundabout just outside Bishops Stortford. I remember this Renault Clio on the inside of me as I cut into the single lane across the front of it. The car then followed me along a dual carriageway and couldn't keep up. This pleased me as it proved that the Smart was capable of beating a Clio if nothing else. I turned off at a roundabout to the sound of a horn beeped rather aggressively and pulled up at the pub. Coming out about an hour later I found some fan mail on my car and judging by the handwriting, the hard looking docker type I had seen driving the Clio was actually a girl! Apparently my driving skills made me akin to a fornicating member or small scratch on your skin usually made by a pin.

I had now picked up another sponsor and at the back of my mind had the confidence to predict to anyone who would listen, including the long-suffering store detective at Tesco, that I would have the final two sponsors by the end of March. My prediction was looking quite favourable by the twentieth as the penultimate sponsor had been obtained. I then received a phone call.

'Hello Dave, have you read the *New York Herald* today?'

You can probably guess my reply but I will tell you anyway. 'No,' I replied.

Well, apparently there was an article about comedy films being released in the summer of 2008 and one of them was a remake of *Get Smart*, the 1960s spoof spy series. Mike, the caller, popped the relevant page in to me and I went to work. Firstly, I tracked down the film company Warner Brothers and within minutes obtained their address in London. I then spent hours trying to transpose the promotional posters of the film onto the photo of my car in order that they would appreciate what the car would look like. Once done I composed a letter and complete with photo, some stickers, and badges, I delivered, within 24 hours of the article appearing in the *New York Herald*, a proposal for my car to be a moving billboard for the film. More than 24 hours after delivering the package I still hadn't heard back. In fact, 12 months later I still haven't heard a thing. The film has now been released and is available on DVD – and I still haven't heard back.

Scouring the internet having done my usual morning routine,

YouTube, zoomzoomsmart, *The Sun*.com etc. I discovered a Mercedes magazine that is published in conjunction with the Mercedes Owners' Club. I contacted the Club to enquire if they would be interested in an article about the Smart and The Cannonball. I received a reply to confirm that they would. I was back! As stated, the whole venture of the car, the rally, the sponsorship, was one hell of a roller-coaster with the highs celebrated with the customary wine and the lows commiserated with the same, the ideas fuelled by the same again. The well-trodden path among my faithful in the Tesco wine aisle was again utilised to the full.

I pounded the streets on the last weekend of March with my 'battle bag' full of leaflets, badges and stickers. I made my way from Kensington through to Piccadilly Circus and intended if possible to visit an old friend, who apparently was still alive and kicking: the 'Chelsea Cruise'. Every last Saturday of the month, custom cars would meet up around Battersea Park and generally cruise the Embankment and round the park. I used to regularly attend in a variety of cars in the late 70s and early to mid-80s and had been told only recently that the event still existed, although on a much smaller scale. I would try to visit. My article for the Mercedes' owners magazine had been emailed so as March was coming to a close, things again were heading in the right direction.

March closed with me attending the Chelsea Cruise and I literally mean 'me attending' as there was no other cars or people. That Saturday proved to be a complete damp squib as I was aiming to put leaflets out around the Kensington area in the hope of attracting the wealthy! However, the perpetual rain left me sitting in the car for most of the day. Nevertheless, April was round the corner and what a lovely girl she is.

April is the fourth month and one of only four months comprising 30 days. April was originally the second month of the year in the Roman calendar until King Numa Pompilius came along in 700 BC and added January and February. *Aperire*, the Latin for April means, 'to open': it is the season when trees and flowers begin to open. It begins with Aries and ends with Taurus.

The advertising was still in full swing with any companies with 'smart' in their titles receiving a request for sponsorship. Five months after the original 'push' of advertising back in November, I was heartened to see that the same old 'ignore the request for sponsorship regime' still existed and that no one replied. The car was virtually finished when I finally managed to get the final sponsor, a lawyers' practice which specialise in child law.

My tactics changed that month. Heartened by the positive response I got with the Mercedes magazine, I approached local magazines and publications and managed to secure three articles in three different ones publicising the event and the car. All these magazines would be distributed in May. One in particular, the South Woodford Village Gazette, proved to be a big help not only running one article but an editorial plus two or three subsequent articles. I decided that May would also see the start of the big London Push with the leaflets that were still sitting patiently in their boxes, approximately 4,000 of them. May would be make or break.

An email was received from Cannonball HQ confirming the venue. I was surprised at my reaction to this as it drove home the fact that the event was most definitely on and I now had a date and a venue: Sandown Park racecourse, Surrey, returning to the Grand Hotel Brighton, six days later.

There was also something that I had put to the back of my mind for some time. Some 3,000 miles in a Smart car: the extent of the journey, the shear bloody length of the thing, equivalent to London to Newcastle approximately ten times or 400 miles short of driving from London to New York. I had put myself in a sort of denial about the whole thing up to that point, concentrating on the more immediate things like work and the pile of leaflets, T-shirts and badges that seemed to be making themselves at home in my conservatory. The forum for The Cannonball was now in full swing, with a few old characters from previous years exchanging banter and new members like myself occasionally chipping in, but on the whole, generally just watching events unfold. Towards the end of April I came to a bit of a halt with everything and joined in a few website forums, including The Cannonball one, and waited for May and the publication of the articles.

May is the fifth month of the year in the Gregorian calendar and one of seven Gregorian months with a length of 31 days. It is also a month within the season of spring in the northern hemisphere, and of autumn in the southern hemisphere. It begins with the sun in the sign of Taurus and ends in the sign of Gemini. It is also said that the month may have been named after the Greek goddess Maia, who was identified with the Roman goddess of fertility.

The first Monday in May was the first of two bank holidays enjoyed in England during this month so I decided to head for Southend-on-Sea. This has been a Mecca of East London and Essex's finest for generations. People religiously head for the coast to proudly show off their cropped hair, bulging stomachs, scars and numerous badly-drawn tattoos with equally bad spelling. All local football teams are equally represented in football tops and, of course, there are the cars. The Renault Clios, Fiat Puntos, Ford Fiesta Zetecs, and numerous Japanese cars, all vie with each other up and down the promenade with various trance and hardcore something blaring out of their windows. Southend is not quite as bad as it seems and it has offered some interesting cars and people over the years, especially in the late 1970s and 1980s. It boasts some popular night spots and in some years, well days, was definitely the place to be seen. Recently, it has started to be regenerated with building work to the old hotels and buildings, including the expansion of the amusement park on the sea front, plus the casino. I arrived on a blazing hot day, especially for May, having had a relatively trouble-free trip down. Driving along the front I found a parking space close to the beach and perfect for exposing the car, being about 50 feet from the entrance to the amusement park. I headed off along the front, weaving in and out of mums (no sign of the dads) with prams, numerous Tottenham, Arsenal, West Ham, and Chelsea fans, God knows how many tons of beer-filled bellies, most of which were turning that pale shade of red conducive with the onset of a proud exposure on Tuesday morning at work. The idea was to give out leaflets, some of which had decided to leave the comfort of the conservatory and join me; however, after ten minutes of wandering around I decided to get something to eat. A café on the front near the pier beckoned and in I went.

'A cheeseburger and chips plus chicken nuggets and chips please.'

'Would you like a drink'?

'Two Cokes thanks.' Just in case you were thinking the obvious (fat bastard), there were two of us, OK?

'OK, just to let you know your food might take a little bit longer as we cook everything fresh here,' said the waitress

'OK,' I replied.

Now I repeated this conversation here for a reason. 'We cook everything fresh here': how can you cook a cheeseburger and chips plus chicken nuggets fresh? Is there someone at the back gently massaging the little bits of freshly slaughtered cow and chicken into burgers and nuggets? Is there someone cutting up potatoes into finely-elongated pieces, to order, all in approximately ten minutes? Unlikely, but still the waitress did seem extremely proud of the fact that everything was fresh!

The rest of the day was spent wandering around and driving about with the car getting quite a few glances. Strangely enough, I returned home with the same number of leaflets I took with me.

My 'rock and roll lifestyle' life saw me two days later in the south of France on business and this led to an embarrassing situation. On leaving Nice quite a classy looking lady got on the plane with a large package and was told that it had to go in the hold. She made a bit of an issue about the fact it was valuable but reluctantly agreed, and while the exchange between her and the steward didn't hold up the flight, it did cause a stir. Two hours later I found myself behind her at immigration and her second clash of the day over her not following the proper route round the cordoned-off area to the customs desk. After her next locking of horns with authority I, in order to appear humorous and understanding, while acknowledging that the UK is not the best place to live at the moment said, 'With a bit of luck they won't let you in.' She gave me a look that could kill exactly at the same time I thought, 'that didn't come out right'. The complimentary zoomzoomsmart sticker I had in my pocket to give her stayed there.

The weather started hot, which was good as it brought people out and people out meant the car being noticed. The feedback I was getting certainly proved the car was being remarked upon, especially in Southend. A couple of people asked me if I was there on bank holiday Monday, as they saw the car. The weeks rolled on with The Cannonball forum gathering momentum and drivers registering from Dubai (the PR work must have paid off!!) Canada, Malta, Belgium, Holland and most of the UK. I began to grasp the seriousness of the event and the other drivers' intent, while also noticing, at the same time, the calibre of the cars growing into an impressive list. My current car would have matched most of the entrants' cars. However I felt that this would have been an easier option to take it and found myself more excited that the Smart was also being noticed more on the forum than I believe my Mercedes would have been. My plans for leaflet distribution were still stumbling mainly due to the rain that perpetually fell from the middle of May to the end of the month. Finally, armed with the battle bag full of leaflets and badges I headed off to Camden Market complete with a mind-numbing hangover, a legacy of my friend's birthday party the night before.

Camden didn't disappoint: pounding reggae music, an assortment of punks and goths, a passing cavalcade of fully dressed to the nines mods on scooters and light drizzle completed a Sunday morning scene. I wandered about with a pounding headache, two bored teenagers and a bag full of leaflets. An hour later I found myself in the food section and had a chicken curry which had the desired effect of semi-clearing my head. With renewed vigour, out came the leaflets and all three of us strode round giving out the said leaflets, only no one wanted them! People just moved away, backing off. It dawned on me that even I, when approached by someone with something in their hand, do likewise, decline the offer and walk on, unless it's a drink, so I was annoyed at myself that I didn't think of that when ordering 5,000 bloody leaflets. It was time to regroup and rethink my strategy as the other thing bothering me was time: it was five weeks to the start.

June is the sixth month in the Gregorian calendar and derives its name from the Roman goddess Juno, wife of Jupiter. June in the northern hemisphere is the equivalent of December in the southern hemisphere. June is actually in spring until the 21st when it becomes summer and, actually, if you get married in June you are in good karma as Juno is the goddess of marriage. On the flip side, it's also Donald Duck's birthday on the 9th.

The beginning of June saw me head north to Nottingham and smarts r us for the service, tune and general last look at the car before the off. I was invited in to watch the service and pick up a few pointers in case of niggling defects on the run. The Smarts' operation in Nottingham is well run and the unit from which they work is a hive of activity with some interesting-looking prototypes lurking in the corners. The briefing from one of the mechanics was concise and thorough as he changed the oil and plugs, showed me where certain access points to the lights and water were etc. I dutifully stood there and listened; however, when referring to the notes I had made later I saw that I had only written 'screwdriver' down. The car, refreshed, revitalised, and fully serviced, promptly broke down! No not really, a little joke there. Off I set past the Radcliffe power station and down onto the M1, a journey that theoretically started this whole odyssey all those months ago. This time the realism of the event and particularly the closeness of it was really dawning on me as I headed south. The car was running well, albeit in the heavy rain, but I still felt secure and safe enough to push the car and it responded perfectly. The journey back to London re-emphasised for me that the car would cope with the first 160 miles of The Cannonball quite well.

My well-travelled route to work, every day, was the M11. The week after the service it had those 'average speed' cameras on it while some workmen were picking up bits of paper or repainting a white line or something equally important, so that the drivers on the M11 could average 53mph and be fined, thereby helping the government recoup some of the billions they have lost. Not wishing to help the government I was cruising in the heart of the 50mph zone on the Friday after the service when alongside me came a Lamborghini Murcielago. As the speed restriction finished he roared off only to get stuck behind a slower vehicle. I found myself behind him in the third lane when he slowly accelerated, building up speed. Gradually his speed increased, and increased to the extent that one of those great moments in life appeared, a Lamborghini in the third lane passing you and right behind it a Smart car, both travelling at a speed that you would certainly notice. It re-emphasised, again, the reason I bought and kept the Smart: it certainly wouldn't have been or looked the same to those weary Friday morning drivers if I were in my Mercedes.

I decided, after a heart to heart with the leaflets, that while they were good company and, no, they didn't take up much room, they really had to go. One of my closest friends that night, a sleek look-ing individual with a nice fine aroma and fruity taste, had been nagging away at me all night about the leaflets, culminating in a very late discussion with the leaflets' representatives and it was decided that the next day they would be dispatched door to door in my local area. They left in two bags and set off on their own little adventures through people's doors. I was also bullish about the car's profile and the gods were also helping. The 21st saw at Brooklands Park the tenth anniversary Smart car meeting, at which there would be hundreds of Smarts in attendance and perhaps a few humans!

Saturday morning, 21 June, started with drizzle, and was not really conducive to an outdoor car show. Undeterred I took the car to a new car wash where no jet wash was but the car lovingly tended with sponges. A jet wash, while thoroughly clearing those stubborn stains, also has the tendency to clear all my sponsorship logos off the car.

They did a really good job and the car was spotless, but unfor-tunately as soon as I drove it out the rain that was falling soon changed all that. I picked up Adrian, my co-driver, and we headed off to Brooklands, a forerunner for the big day two weeks later as the start of The Cannonball was at Sandown Park, merely a few miles down the road from Brooklands. Through the Dartford tunnel on the M25 and we began to pick up some other Smarts on their way. The reaction to us was really good with other drivers beeping their childish horns, and then realising their acute embarrassment and reverting to flashing their lights and waving. We in turn waved back, ignoring the horn completely, the sign of an experienced Smart driver! The journey went surprisingly quickly and comfortably. We pulled into the event heading straight to the smarts r us stand, where the car would remain for the day.

Armed with the leaflets that remained from the house to house operation, Adrian and myself managed to dispose of the rest of them on most of the cars in the car park and sadly that was it – the last of the leaflets had gone; my little friends had gone on their own journey, their adventure of sorts. We wandered round what was a good show, seeing all sorts of Smarts and handing out badges and stickers. The Brooklands museum and track is now wholly Mercedes-based, with a very interesting museum and showroom showing the history of the car and track.

Brooklands was the world's first purpose-built motor racing track constructed in 1907 and initially a 2.75-mile course which had two large 30ft banked sections and was in places up to 100ft wide. In its first year, Selwyn Francis Edge drove a green 6-cylinder Napier on an endurance 24-hour circuit covering a mammoth 1,581miles averaging 66mph. Don't forget, we in two weeks time were going 3,000 miles in five days trying to average 61mph. Easy! Except Mr Edge didn't have traffic, cities, towns, tractors and people to contend with. Incidentally, the 3,000 mile figure is approximately the distance travelled by the cars in the Le Mans 24-hour car endurance.

Brooklands was host a few years later in 1913 to one Percy Lambert who reached a record speed of 103.84mph: the first car to exceed 100mph. After promising his fiancée that he would stop, he did what every bloke would do and did it again. He tried unsuccessfully to beat the record and unfortunately died in one attempt. Not content with that, Percy, complete with full racing overalls, has been seen wandering around the grounds of Brooklands ever since. Interestingly, the last speed attempt and record at Brooklands was carried out by Kenelm Lee Guinness (yes, he was related to the black stuff people) who drove a 350hp Sunbeam at 135.37mph. The car was subsequently sold to Malcolm Campbell and became his first *Bluebird*. Not only does the museum give a fascinating insight into the history of motor racing, but you also have a chance to drive on the track and the wet track.

Situated in the showroom on our visit in its own section was the new Brabus Smart, the ultimate 112 with its very own price tag of €45,000, hopefully to capitalise on 112 mad multi-millionaires who just happened to attend the show. While it is a good looking car the price tag was causing a stir among the people looking at it. It was pointed out that the car was one of 112; personally at that price I would prefer it to be one of one. Having wandered round the Mercedes showroom and been asked to leave for giving out zoom-zoomsmart badges and stickers, we found ourselves wandering back to the smarts r us stand when, out of the blue, a girl dressed as Maid Marion jumped out and asked if we would like to go into a tent with her where she would show us something! Disappointed, five minutes later, we were out having been given a tour of the new Mercedes Viano.

Time to leave Brooklands and having said goodbye to the Smarts r us team we headed back round the M25 to Essex and again the car showed the vast difference between itself and a lot of the 'normal Smarts' that were also heading our way on the motorway.

Two weeks to go to the big day and apart from work the car front was quietening down, so much so, and having sold my other car, I decided to hire a car and keep the Smart off the road in case someone crashed into it. I hired a Chevy 57 Belair relative called a Chevy Kalos. The 1.2 litre engine was poor but it filled a gap and that's about it. The Cannonball forum was getting busier with the previous year's competitors vying with each other, the new competitors asking pertinent questions and me just messing around. The main themes through the forum were the hours, or lack of them, for getting sleep, the speed element, the provisions being taken, and the electrical equipment being installed. We at 'Team Smart' had no electrical equipment whatsoever – alarm bells, if fitted, would have been ringing. As previously mentioned, I am good at getting myself out of situations that if I was half as good at anticipating I would never be in in the first place and The Cannonball was quickly becoming one. No spare tyre, no sat nav, no radar warning devices, no tools, no emergency provisions, the only contribution a £15.99 Tesco European driving kit which I found by chance at the end of the mother of all aisles 'the wine aisle', and three packets of sports mixture sweets. Bring it on.

Saturday 5 July 2008 had arrived after months and months of leaflets, badges, stickers, emails and T-shirts. Containing my excitement I went into work on the Saturday morning and finished off a few bits that needed doing, then headed home via my new good mates at the multi-storey car park for a quick 'brush up and clean' before meeting Adrian at 5 p.m. I had had eight months to get ready for this and at 5 p.m. I was still at home packing. With all the rushing around, packing was something I had completely forgotten about. Yes I know I was about to embark on a 3,000-mile journey round Europe and had completely missed the fact that there were no overnight or luggage bags in the car! So there I was rapidly throwing stuff into a bag when I should have already been at the first point of the trip. Arriving at Adrian's I found him completely ready and within five minutes we were ready to push on, but not before Adrian then pointed out that he had never driven a Smart car before and should he at least have a go now?

9

We are Cannonballers

On arrival we parked up next to a Lotus Elise and a Subaru, unpacked and headed into the plush entrance hall and checked in to the Oatlands Hotel. The hotel itself was built on the site of the royal palace of Henry VIII. Oatlands became a hotel in 1856 with a Mr Peppercorn becoming its first manager and boasts feature rooms with four-poster beds which thankfully our room didn't have. Our room shrugged its shoulders and pointed at a couple of single ones a healthy distance apart for two red-blooded racing driver men like ourselves.

'Cannonballers?' said the receptionist.

'Yes we are,' we responded. 'Yes-we-are!'

'OK,' he replied fairly non-plussed. 'What car are you doing it in?' he ventured.

'A Smart car,' came the reply. The non-plussed receptionist soon became very plussed. 'A Smart car?'

'Yep,' we replied in unison. A look that we were to get used to came over his face. I called it 'admiration'; however Adrian saw it as it really was: 'Do I call security? And how quickly can I distance myself from these nutters.' Filling in the forms and collecting our keys, all at arms length, we went and found our room. Unpacking our bags we immediately left the room and headed downstairs to the lobby and were directed by our newly-plussed friend to the terrace where the other 'proper' Cannonballers were.

'Smart car.'

Silence fell on the gathering. Yes, we had done it again. 'Feckin

73

hell you really are doing it in a Smart car,' said Irish Dave as the rest of the Cannonballers took a collective step back.

'Yes and it's outside,' I ventured. The ice was well and truly broken and what should have been an early night was well and truly accompanied into the early hours by Mr Artois and Mrs Stella and filled with brilliant driving stories and tales from previous years, plus guesses as to what would happen this year. We were joined at one point by Darren who wasn't staying at the hotel but lived nearby and was taking part with his mate Dean, driving a Vauxhall. He joined the conversation on one of the popular topics: where we might be going. I remember saying that it must be northern Europe with parts of eastern Europe; bearing in mind previous rallies it was a no brainer really. He headed off and we all soon retired to our rooms.

A hearty full English breakfast started a rainy overcast Sunday and we soon had the car packed and headed off. Out of the hotel left down the road to the petrol station to fill up and then right out of the petrol station to the roundabout, left again, then . . . ?

'We're going the wrong way.'

'Right, what way then?'

'Turn round and back that way.' Ten minutes later we were driving back past the petrol station, headed into the hotel and started again. The omens weren't looking good. We couldn't even find Sandown Park five miles away. Tesco appeared like a beacon to our plight and we pulled in. The wine aisle did prove tremendous pull for me as I went in but I resisted the chance to be unfaithful and managed to find the books and magazine section. The newly-acquired *European Road Map* (£9.99) didn't really seem concise enough for Weybridge to Sandown. The map and directions given to us by Cannonball we couldn't understand, not because they weren't good enough; it was just we couldn't understand them. However, the good old-fashioned leaning out the window and asking a local trick paid off, it's just we didn't expect to do it so early on the trip and in English.

Sandown Park is situated in a fairly affluent part of Surrey and was built in 1875 in favour of a lunatic asylum which was planned in its place. It boasts the fact that it was the Queen Mother's favourite racecourse and is home to a plethora of Blue Ribbon race meetings. On opening, it had the distinction of being the first enclosed racecourse in the land and was described as 'a place where a gentleman could take his ladies without fear of them hearing coarse language and witnessing uncouth behaviour'. Something, I fear, if he had got a lift with his ladies in a Smart car that Sunday morning, he wouldn't have been able to avoid!

If you ever find yourself standing in the main stand watching the racing and your 100:1 bet is coming up on the rails to almost pass the 3:4 on favourite with 100 yards to go and you can't bear to watch then, on a clear day, raise your eyes and look north where you will see Wembley Stadium. Incredibly, Wembley is visible from Sandown Park 17 miles away.

Flustered, we arrived to then have to negotiate with the security guard on the gate who first tried to usher us into the 'spectator parking' and after finally convincing him we were actually driving in the event gave us a manly look of admiration and waved us through. Parking up among the mightily impressive-looking cars, the enormity of what we had entered hit us. Yes, there were Ferraris, Lamborghinis, Porsches, Aston Martins – the list went on and on – but there amongst them was the Smart and, more importantly, our intention to compete. Just pulling up and parking was the first step and soon whispers and nudges abounded as people noticed the little car, and then began taking pictures and asking questions. The Smart had arrived and was generating interest. We headed over to the check-in desk and collected our 'competitor badges'. On to another desk, where we deposited our dinner suits for the final-night party 50 miles away in Brighton. A form was given to us to be completed for a Brittany ferry crossing from Portsmouth to Caen. A clue! Mingling and giving the impression that I was driving one of the Ferraris I bumped into Darren. 'You look tired,' I said.

'Of course, I've been up all night loading the sat nav and computer with road maps and for eastern Europe and Scandinavia after our chat last night. Three bloody hours it took so I've had no sleep.'

'Oh right,' I sheepishly replied. 'Anyway, better go and check the car.' I walked away hiding the Brittany ferry form. 'Talin here we come!' came the shout as he walked up the steps to the check-in.

We mingled, chatting and watching Chris, a nightclub photographer who drove a Smart, and someone I had met through my brother-in-law Russell, take pictures of the cars and before long we were ushered to a drivers' briefing, where Jan the organiser told us the rules and regulations, the dos and don'ts, and a couple of stories about previous years' events to give us something to think about. The good advice was to remove all stickers and referencing to the race apart from a small, simple 'You've just been Cannonballed' sticker on the back of the car. I looked at the Smart with its Union Jack livery and numerous sponsor stickers, and expected the worst. Resigned now to a hassle-full trip with all of Europe's police picking on the only car that looked as if it was doing a rally, I was pleased I packed the master plan. I had printed off three letters, one from Riccione in Italy, one from Cadiz in Spain and a third from Artus in Denmark, all inviting us to Smarticus 08, a fictitious Smart car event that we would be going to rather than doing The Cannonball. I would show the relevant one to the police, if stopped. All we had to do now was to get in the car, get ready, start the car and avoid Darren.

10

Gentlemen, Start Your Engines

Recipe for Sunday Brunch

Firstly take a respected racecourse in Surrey and add a fine drizzle. Once lightly dampened, add a good selection of car buffs with the odd fanatic and place them round the edges. Over a period of two hours slowly filter in a selection of American muscle cars, a good handful of Italian sports cars, some Japanese fast cars, a few Germanic beasts (not too many as they tend to spoil the dish), a couple of British thoroughbreds, and a soupçon of German quirky engineering.

Allow ingredients to simmer and stand for about 110 minutes and then allow the engines to start.

Step back and let the dish overflow with a stunning soundtrack of the world's finest cars all making their presence felt the only way they can. Try not to allow yourself to be too disappointed that the little soupçon of Smart is not immediately noticed, as the benefit of adding this will be noticed later.

'Are we on the right road?'

'Yes.'

'You sure?'

'For God's sake, we've only been on the road five minutes.'

'I know but I can't see any signs for Portsmouth or the A3.' This was the conversation for the first five minutes of The Cannonball.

We pulled up at the start and Adrian jumped out to collect Mission Pack Number 1. Sitting in the driver's seat I glanced around and noticed 'the look' from quite a few of the spectators and couldn't help seeing a collective step back as I caught their eyes and smiled. Adrian jumped in and we roared off.

'It must be this way, just keep going,' said Adrian, having eventually seen a sign for the A3 and Portsmouth, drama number one out of the way.

Having opened the Mission Pack, a daunting 1,125 miles to Sintra, which is located about 20 miles from Lisbon, faced us. 'That's miles,' I said, and all we could do was laugh nervously. I must admit, after all my self-induced hype about eastern Europe and Scandinavia I felt a little pang of disappointment that we weren't actually going there, but that went almost as quickly as it came. I did wonder what Darren thought. As we hit the main roundabout taking us to the A3 and Portsmouth we saw Adrian and Kevin in their Subaru on the side of the road. I managed with a great deal of professional driving to slow our beast down from nearly 25mph to a complete stop next to them. We jumped out to offer assistance and it would seem the engine management system was playing up, causing the car to misfire; a shame as they had only gone a few miles. Honestly speaking, I was struggling with the terminology between Adrian, and Adrian and Kevin, so I was reluctant to touch anything and therefore took the option of standing between the cars and the road and waving at people driving past. Adrian and Kevin were soon confident enough to push on to Portsmouth and we headed off down the A3. I was now phoning, hands-free of course, everyone and telling them the destination. I spoke to a couple of mates, Dickie and Pete, who had been to the Essex 'polio' (as it's pronounced in Essex) meeting the day before, who told me that unlike the polo events elsewhere in the UK, Essex didn't want to disappoint and true to form a pitch battle started with tables, chairs and bottles flying amongst the fists and boots. They couldn't tell me what started it as they were too pissed but seem to think it was probably over a bloke! Now in case you think that 'polio' in Essex attracts numerous homosexuals or a couple of 'pals' were helping someone out, you would be wrong: the mass brawl seemed to be a ladies-only event, and with visions of scantily-clad Essex girls brawling in a field with horses and riders with huge mallets clobbering everything in sight, made the journey to the docks at Portsmouth fly by.

We arrived at the docks immediately behind a Ferrari 430 Spider and a blue TVR and pulled up in our allotted lane ready for the crossing. The drivers already there were greeting the new ones and immediately the excited chatter of Portugal and beyond was underway. As we chatted, more cars arrived and so the chatter grew. A few sporadic bystanders and an assortment of lorry drivers were joining the throng, having been drawn by the steady procession of supercars entering into the docks on a drizzly Sunday afternoon. Thankfully it wasn't long before Adrian and Kevin arrived in their slightly ill-running Subaru. They joined the throng of jabbering people, selected a few of them and again this strange language was being spoken about 'brains of the car', 'engine management' etc. I took this as an opportunity to move on and decided to wave at people again and smile. It wasn't long before I too was chatting to a couple of very nice French seamen from the ferry, who had obviously spotted me waving. I was back with Adrian and the others with the strange language quite quickly as there had obviously been a terrible misunderstanding due to my French not being as good as it should have been. Sensing an advantage over the others I asked my new French friends if they could get me on the boat quickly (so I would be at the front to get off first). Unfortunately, this translated into 'Could you have me on the boat quickly and can I get off first?' Apparently they didn't have a problem with both.

The slow procession of cars started to climb the ramp to the boat with a few of them with lower suspensions having to weave their way up to avoid grounding out. No such problems with the Smart as we zoomed up the slope only to be told to slow down and probably as a punishment for this, or for leading on two of the staff, we were ushered to the top ramp, thereby being one of the last off. The boat slowly moved off and we headed out of Portsmouth on a blustery Sunday afternoon for a six-hour crossing. Now I hate boats at the best of times, and really don't make the best sailor, so six hours on this boat didn't appeal. However, the adrenalin rush of the event helped me get through the first half an hour of the journey. True to form, as we left the relative calm confines of the port, the boat started to move about a bit more and I headed to the back and the open deck to take in gulps of fresh rain-soaked air. Obviously realising my plight, Roger Federer and Rafael Nadal decided to play a scintillating four-set game of tennis at Wimbledon and to prolong it even more let the rain interrupt it, thereby allowing me to sit rigidly in my seat and stare at the game while trying to ignore the perpetual rocking motion of the boat.

Caen, situated in northern France, is the gateway to the sumptuous delights of Normandy and Brittany and also home to the port of Ouistreham which also doubles up as a seaside town. Caen itself boasts the fact that it was William the Conqueror's favourite city – so much so that he married his cousin Matilda of Flanders there and was then promptly excommunicated by the Pope because of it. While on the subject of scandal, outrageous behaviour and sexual adventures, something was slowly coming out of the inky darkness of the Channel toward the extremely quiet and slightly damp seaside town. It approached at a steady pace and ploughed right down the middle of the town, only stopping to be tied up. Cannonball had arrived at 10.30 on dark rain-filled night in seaside France.

An arduous two hours after Roger and Rafael had given up at Wimbledon followed and I eventually found myself at the front of the ferry in the restaurant, grappling with a ham baguette and Coke and aimlessly staring at some twinkling lights in the distance. My ordeal was almost over and land beckoned. Buoyed by this, I had decided to have something to eat as a long haul lay ahead of us. Having finished the baguette without any of it returning, we docked and I made my way to the car, not far, as it was on the level below my deck, not the level that led directly off the boat. Sitting in the car the engines below fired into life, Ferraris and Lambos making the most of the acoustics of a cross-Channel ferry. Slowly they disembarked, again some of them snaking over the ramps to avoid grounding out, and then the lorries slowly moving off, followed by the cars, Winnebagos, caravanettes, vans, the two poor sods on a 1960s Vespa, some more cars, and even more lorries.

'Half the cars will be in Spain by now,' I moaned as we sat in our elevated position waiting for the lower decks to clear. Finally, we started our engines and edged forward.

'Where the hell could he have gone?' It was 25 minutes since the cars started leaving and some idiot, two cars ahead, still hadn't got to his car. Not even eight hours into The Cannonball and I was stressed. Finally, 'lightning' turned up, started his engine and we edged off the boat and on to terra firma or Ouistreham as the locals call it. It was a dark, damp, depressing scene with a desolate small fairground and few sparsely-lit shops with a few locals sitting around – why I don't know, perhaps they had completely given up and couldn't even raise the enthusiasm to go home. They were, however, rewarded for their apathy with the glorious sight of most Cannonballers heading through the now congested streets leading away from the port. We found ourselves behind a Bentley, TVR and Mustang and slowly moved out of town looking for signs for Lisbon, or if not the A28, which would take us south. Before the A28 we hit the road between Ouistreham and Caen with Adrian driving as he used to live this side of France near Bordeaux and therefore knew the roads. In a small convoy we headed, at speed, toward Caen, illuminating the night sky by way of a speed camera located just outside the port which was akin to the paparazzi outside a nightclub, with the flashes going off every few seconds as we and numerous Cannonballers flew through. Rather than sticking to the main road and noting it was 11.30 at night we took the decision to cut through Conde Sur Noireau and Flers, as who would be out at that time of night? Our hunch seemed good, especially in Conde Sur Noireau and we travelled through at speeds we probably shouldn't have and pushed on to Flers in good spirits.

Flers was bigger than the previous town and had 'traffic lights'. 'Go on, go through them,' I said, but Adrian stood firm and we waited. At green we were off to find ourselves stuck behind the last person in France to be on their Sunday drive at 25 to 30mph and with no room to overtake. I felt my patience waning. Bloody traffic lights again, and a further couple of kilometres behind three people in an old Renault who seemed intent on taking in the views at midnight in a deserted town. All this time my mind was working overtime imagining how far all the other cars had got. Finally we overtook them, picking up a reasonable speed and thankfully it wasn't long before signs for Alencon and the A28 appeared. We found the A28 and immediately picked up speed to a suitable cruising speed and settled down for what was rapidly appearing to be a long drive to Lisbon. The shear blackness of the French countryside engulfed us as we sped past numerous juggernauts that seemed to dominate the roads and, in particular, the inside lane at that time of night. Having not seen any other car from The Cannonball, and bearing in mind the calibre of the other cars, we resigned ourselves that we were in last place and again pushed on. Soon a sign appeared for Le Mans and for someone who knew the roads in these parts Adrian asked a strange question.

'Do we head for Le Mans or not?'

'Don't you know?' I ventured. 'You lived round here.'

He pointed out that he in fact lived 400km south near Bordeaux. I got out our only source of reference, the £9.99 map of Europe and looked up our location. Now 11 hours into The Cannonball, I realised another failing in our scantily prepared survival kit: no torch. The tiny interior light located at our knees didn't help when trying to study a map, so until we found a petrol station or street light we were in the dark, so to speak. Le Mans was upon us and the decision was taken to stay on the A28 and head for Tours. The roads were perfect for a good speed slightly in excess of the speed limit but apart from the trucks, there appeared to be nothing else on the road. So with a backdrop of a 1970's disco CD we headed on. The adrenalin of the whole thing prohibited sleep so the ideal scenario of one driver asleep and one driving really looked like it wouldn't happen. I took to staring at the blackness, the intermittent headlights coming in the other direction, deciding whether to stop and fit the headlight deflectors, which we had forgotten to do, leading to every lorry going in the opposite direction flashing us to tell us to. After a while I noticed something in the mirror behind us: headlights were approaching and gaining rapidly. We were hovering around the 90mph mark but these lights were closing in at an alarming rate.

'Ade, looks like the police are behind us.'

He glanced in the rear-view mirror and instinctively slowed to 80mph. Within seconds there was the sound of a horn, a rush of air and noise. A yellow flash went past causing us to literally to rock in its wake. The yellow 500-plus horsepower Mustang shot past us and as quickly as it was upon us was gone. Welcome to Cannonball, our first real encounter, and we were literally blown away.

'I thought we were last,' I said.

'Probably are now,' said Adrian.

*

Bordeaux was upon us and offered lights to read by and petrol stations to fill up at. We had met the Mustang again, in fact we passed it as it was filling up at a petrol station; he in turn had passed us and we met up at another petrol station. Were we vying for last place? We had yet to see any of the other 40 cars. Bordeaux offered to me the first 'mental' hurdle. Unfortunately we could not, nor had time to, pick up a few bottles of wine, therefore cutting out the wine trafficker known as Tesco's. Pulling out of the service station we headed on to the E70 and headed south to Biarritz, and waited for the sun to put in an appearance. Speeding south we suddenly got a flash from a camera almost at the same time as a black Porsche went past us with a toot and wave. Cannonball car two on our travels. Then the sight that brings fear: blue lights flashing and closing rapidly.

'Ade, looks like the police are behind us.'

He glanced in the mirror and instinctively slowed to 40mph, this time in order to avoid careering into the back of a flat-bodied truck that had suddenly appeared in front of us.

The police roared past us, leaving us relieved on two counts, the latter, the fact that the truck was still in one piece. About a mile down the road we saw the Porsche pulled over with two police officers standing beside it.

Heading to Biarritz the sun was beginning to break through and after another quick stop I took over the driving and we headed towards Spain and the sunshine.

Heading down the A63 toward the Spanish border the sun was up and the road began to get busier. The car was beginning to get noticed, with many a vehicle occupant and lorry driver straining to get a better glimpse of us. Other than the Mustang and the Porsche, we had yet to see any other car from The Cannonball and wondered what the night had bought for them and where they all were. A story related by a few seasoned 'Ballers' on the boat referred to a previous year when a Ferrari and a Porsche were stopped for speeding in France and subsequently, on being stopped a second time, promptly had their cars confiscated, only to find them put in an auction where they were told they could buy them back. Had anyone this year suffered a similar fate?

With the day getting lighter and the car still running well, we counted down the kilometres to the second country and soon hit Spain. On entering the country, we saw the Dubai Ferrari and tucked in behind them to find Jan the organiser in her Audi behind us. The wonder of the event was beginning to grow: we had travelled through the night and quite a few hundred kilometres, convinced that most of the cars were streaks ahead, only to find ourselves behind one of the fastest cars on the run and just in front of the organiser.

The next big town we passed through was Irun, and in trying to keep up with the Ferrari we enjoyed a high speed trail through the early morning traffic on the windy dual carriageway that passed the outskirts of the city. Even after a long night's driving no effects of tiredness were noticed by either of us – in fact Adrian seemed to be enjoying the 100mph-plus chase through the traffic as only a nervous passenger in a Smart car could, with various outbursts of screaming for me to slow down or in some cases, stop. I chose to ignore him, reminding him of the traffic lights in Flers.

Petrol raised its ugly head again and the Ferrari and Jan pulled in to refuel while we pushed on, now at a more sedate speed. Refuelling ourselves we headed to San Sebastian and after convincing myself we were nearly there, I saw that we still had the whole of Spain to pass through before crossing into Portugal.

Clockwise from top: (1) That's the way to sponsor. February, and the blank panels meet Mr Popular! (2) Nice hand writing for a huge docker. (3) The night before bizarrely parked next to the Lotus we would finish directly behind. Note the bird killer's Audi.

You ARE A FUCKING PRICK!

Anti-clockwise from top: (1) Portsmouth docks (2) A bad picture of Adrian, but thankfully we caught Andy, last year's winner, in the background. (3) Italians everywhere

Above: Down that road to the best country in the world. Below: Waiting patiently in line.

Clockwise from top: (1) The Spanish policeman making out he is busy. (2) Look, a full tank of petrol. (3) Channel Tunnel, the end.

11

Eusebio is not Portuguese

The roads in Spain were turning out to be a real joy: empty and in good condition, which proved conducive to a good average speed. The sun was rising and so was the heat, but more importantly the Smart seemed to be revelling in the long empty roads and we managed to keep to a constant 90mph for long stretches. My experience of Spain is really limited to a stag weekend in Marbella, a weekend in Madrid and a weekend in Barcelona, and I was generally surprised at the quiet, barren scenery that was passing us by. My coordination had also deserted me and while I had a road map and The Cannonball Mission Pack to go by, I couldn't grasp exactly where our route was taking us. Added to this I had yet to see a road sign for Madrid or Barcelona, one of which I was convinced we would have to pass through.

The Monday morning was now in full flow and our hour count was 29 hours with no sleep. We had gone from a drizzly Sunday morning to a Sunny desolate midday in the back of beyond in Spain and still the Smart marched on, taking every bump, bend, lorry, ogling local in its stride. We felt even more isolated and, yes, obviously, last, as no other Cannonball car was in sight nor had been seen for a good while. My confidence that we were going in the right direction was at an all-time low, plus for every minute we kept going I realised that we were getting further away from home, and that the possible breakdown recovery service I thought I had would be stretched to find us, let alone get us back. That was, obviously, if I *had* one, which I would check as soon as I got to the next hotel.

We passed through Burgos, which has the third largest cathedral in Spain, but even more importantly was home to another of my good friends from back home. We were now in the La Rioja region and memories came flooding back of the wine aisle in Tesco and the way that many a bottle that had struggled to leave this land for a better life in the UK subsequently ended up in a bottle bank in Harlow. Another familiar sight was greeting us as we headed out of Burgos and that was road signs for Madrid, 240km away, but away in the wrong direction, nevertheless a familiar sight. We pushed on toward Salamanca and the Portuguese border thereafter. Moving closer to Portugal our spirits rose and the foot went down; now averaging 90–95mph we were ticking off the kilometres and heading for unknown territory. I had not been to Portugal and in fact the only famous people we could come up with were Cristiano Ronaldo the footballer, Figo the footballer, Eusebio the footballer – you can now see the level of conversation we were having. The only other famous Portuguese person we could think of in an hour and half of driving was Vasco de Gama, an explorer and possibly a footballer in his spare time. Eusebio wasn't even technically Portuguese as he was, in fact, born in Mozambique.

Eagerly waiting for Portugal to approach we were suddenly passed at great speed by Darren and Dean in their Vauxhall, of all the cars in all of Europe. Once past us, they slowed down to pull into a petrol station into which we followed. Jumping out to fill up they told us of a few technical problems their car was having while I told them that Ronaldo and Figo are both Portuguese. We were deep in conversation when something happened that could have been a forerunner for later in the trip. Having filled the Smart up I went to pay, leaving Darren and Dean at the pump. After paying, when I got back to the car we found ourselves hemmed in by a Spanish police car which didn't move; nor did the police get out. There was just enough room to get by. We edged round them slowly, expecting a knock on the car or for them to stop us, but no. Darren had obviously spotted them and pulled away from the pump in a less exuberant manner than normal and we, having gingerly negotiated our way round, headed off with them following us for a few miles.

The border between Spain and Portugal is at the end of the A62 and you are met by a small town which ironically looks like a South American settlement, which given the history between Spain and Portugal and that part of the world, really isn't really surprising. We slowed down to a walking pace to take in the scenery, and two student types walked out into the road. At first they appeared to be young customs officers as they were wearing florescent-type vests and carrying clipboards. We duly stopped. They were in fact collecting for a charity and managed to get a few euros from us. 'Portugal: the best country in the world,' one of them proclaimed as if he actually believed it, when we pulled away.

'No, we haven't got time,' said Adrian: I was in favour of pulling up again and explaining that we had spent at least an hour and a half discussing Portugal and could only come up with a few footballers and an explorer, and even then one of the footballers was from Mozambique, so how the hell could Portugal be the best country in the world?

The next big town we passed was Guarda, which is the highest town in the country and soon some famous names started to appear on the road signs, Porto and Lisbon. The roads were proving to be equally as good as the Spanish highways and my initial fear that they would be uneven and slow was certainly not the case. Gathering speed we again watched the kilometres disappear as the road spread out in front of us. Our speed was up, in fact we pushed the Smart harder than ever. A mixture of anxiousness to get there and a complete trust in the car was now affecting my driving, so it was with gay abandon that on seeing a slight hump in the road I decided to hit it at speed.

'What was that?' Adrian shouted as we hit the ground and skidded halfway across the road with the dashboard lighting up and a loud bang ringing in our ears.

'I just got all four wheels off the ground,' I said. 'It feels like we've blown a tyre.'

The car certainly wasn't running as smoothly as it had been a few seconds previously. We were a very long way from home and I had blown a tyre, yet I felt no panic. This was Cannonball! Seconds later, however, I was cursing and regretting my *Dukes of Hazzard* imitation. The dual carriageway we were on didn't seem to have a hard shoulder, so we sort of parked half on and half off.

'What do we have to do? Put the fucking triangle out and wear the silly luminous jacket?' I said.

A calmer Adrian just suggested we get out of the car and inspect the damage. I got out and saw that the tyres on my side were not damaged. Adrian got out of the passenger door and saw that neither tyre on his side were damaged. The relief was plain to see as while we were parked in a precarious position, which was also compounded by the fact that we had neither a jack nor a spare wheel, we didn't need them and we would be back on the road in seconds. We set off with a banging coming from the car, so in order to get to where we were going we kept the speed down to a sedate 60mph, taking note to avoid all humps and potholes in the road

Road travel is similar to a long airline flight when, after a good few hours in the air, the final hours and distance seem to pass relatively quickly compared to the first three-quarters of the flight. Even with the added worry of a banging car which clearly had something wrong with it, we soon found ourselves in the vicinity of Sintra. Heading into the region along the N9, having successfully driven 1,100 miles, all we had to do was to follow the instructions in the Mission Pack. Adrian, to be fair, had said on the ferry that we should take some time to study this bit as there were discrepancies between the Mission Pack and what was shown on our £9.99 road map. I in turn said we should leave it until we got there as how hard could it be to find a hotel? Exiting the N9 at what we thought to be Junction 8, as advised, we headed off the motorway and on to the B roads with the added soundtrack of an electrical-come-grinding noise from the front of the car every time we turned the wheel and braked. Not to worry, as when we got to the hotel we would look into it. We found that firstly the N9 on the instructions was in fact the A9 on our road map. This had put us off route to a certain extent: however, not disheartened we went about trying to find the Penha Longa Hotel and Golf Resort in good spirits, as according to our calculations we were only a few kilometres from it and a cold beer, after 32 hours on the road.

'That noise is getting worse and where the fuck is this hotel?' 'How many more times are we going to go past that fucking sign?' 'Bollocks to this, I'm checking into the next place I see.' As you can see the few kilometres turned into almost two hours of driving round that rather picturesque area, well and truly lost.

The phone went.

'David?' It was one of the checkpoint girls asking if we were OK as everyone else was there and we had been spotted on the side of the road after our *Dukes of Hazzard* stunt. It transpired that at the time of the call we weren't too far from the hotel and if we headed into town everyone knew the golf course and would be able to direct us.

Well a rather dopy student didn't know where it was, and neither did the old couple, the single guy walking out of the station, the old guy standing at the side of the road, the two young girls, the other old guy we approached, or the young couple with a dog.

'No one knows this place,' I told HQ at the hotel and was passed on to the receptionist who then tried to guide us in, all the time my mobile bill clocking up and up. After arriving in the region approximately two hours earlier we finally arrived at the hotel with the car grinding and squealing for good effect.

The Penha Longa Hotel and Golf Resort originated in the sixteenth century and was used by the Portuguese royal family. Nestled in the hills of the southern Sintra Mountains it is a short drive from there to Cascais, Lisbon and the picturesque Estoril coast, most of which we had already seen on our way to the hotel. The place offered a peaceful retreat, a glorious swimming pool, an excellent golf course and accommodation; however, more important than any of that, a bar with beer.

Having parked the Smart in the underground car park and

arranged for 1,200 miles of grime, dust, dirt and sweet wrappers to be removed, the immediate concern of the brakes and grinding noise was forgotten as the lure of a pint beckoned. Lager in hand we walked to the outside terrace by the pool where the Cannon-ballers were camped and I was immediately struck by the genuine welcome and concern, plus joy, from the other drivers. It seemed that the Smart was getting a little fan club going which we compounded by firstly getting the car to Portugal and secondly injuring it and *still* getting there. Completely forgetting the fact that Portugal is an hour behind Spain and therefore the same time as London, we immediately made up an hour that I thought we had lost 'exploring' the surrounding area. My dark mood had lifted with the aid of a few pints, a shower, and a few more pints. The Cannon-ball Run is definitely something more than a straight drag across Europe, as that night proved.

We headed to the open-air restaurant at the hotel on a particularly cold night and enjoyed good food and wine plus excellent company including Jamie and his girlfriend Anisa, who had arrived in their BMW at about 11 in the morning, averaging over 90mph for the whole journey. They were followed by a few more drivers who spoke about their journeys. Neil and Mark, in their stunning Jaguar XKR, had not yet made it, having had a blowout in Bordeaux and trouble sourcing one of the mammoth 20in tyres. News was that they would rejoin us later on the Run.

We had a lot to do to keep up in the race. Was the Smart the right car to bring? Still we were there and that was it. The word was spreading that the next day would be track day, as Estoril race track was only three miles away. Armed with this information Adrian and I decided to leave the Smart's woes behind and head off to the nightclub laid on for us and the other drivers. Again, the spirit of The Cannonball was hugely evident with offers of help and equipment plentiful from the other competitors, especially Steve and Frank in the Mazda. The nightclub in all honesty wasn't what we really expected and it wasn't long before the coach that took us there was recalled to pick us up. The cold snap that was affecting

Lisbon at that time was certainly not conducive to an outside night-club, plus our tiredness brought on by the drive meant we needed only one thing: sleep.

We had to be ready at 9.30 the next morning and after a hearty breakfast we headed out of the car park to the front of the hotel, squealing and grinding our way to join the queue of cars that was forming. As we thought, today was track day at the Estoril circuit. We drove in convoy to the track so we couldn't get lost.

Estoril was, up to 1996, a regular on the Formula 1 circuit, however it now plays a big part in the Moto GP calendar. Built in 1972 it was known as the 'Fernada Piers de Silva Circuit' and during the Formula 1 days was best remembered for the world championship decider between Alain Prost and Nikki Lauder in 1984, won by Alain Prost and, a year later, Ayrton Senna's first win. It was also the track which saw Riccardo Patrese's famous airborne backflip after rear-ending Gerhard Berger. The track is known for its low average speed primarily due to the introduction of the Variante Chicane, which is the slowest corner on the GP circuit and forces drivers to drop to first gear, as with another three corners on the circuit. For the anoraks amongst you, the track is made up of ten right-hand corners and four left – something, unless we repaired the Smart, we would not experience.

The convoy worked, and we found the circuit without getting lost, parking up in the pit lane. Getting out, we ambled over to the track. The pressing issue now was the car and the increasingly louder noise coming from it but at least we were at a racing circuit with mechanics, level ground and – more importantly – nowhere to go for a good few hours. First things first: a pep talk from our 'tame racing driver' Phiroze Bilimona, the British GT driver, who advised us on the good etiquette of racing driving and the relevant safety issues, which bearing in mind Estoril's history on safety was a very good idea. However, much of this went in one ear and out the other, because my main concern was our sick car in the pit lane.

The other drivers left the briefing, fired up their engines and set off for an introductory single lap of the track. Poor forlorn Smart sat there like a lonely child left out of a game of football while all the other kids played on, having a good time. By the time our Cannonball colleagues returned to the pit lane, we had jacked the Smart up and discovered that the origin of the noise was a dangerously low brake pad. So, with the cause identified all we had to do was source some pads. Making enquiries with all we discovered a Mercedes dealership not too far from the track. Problem finally solved.

We headed off. First stop, a petrol station to fill up and ask directions. Now I don't know if all Portuguese are like this; however, on asking for directions to the dealership one of the two attendants came bounding out of the kiosk and proceeded to spend almost five minutes pointing and advising us of the route. Not content with that he then went back into the shop and spent a further ten minutes drawing a very detailed map showing the route there and back. Our reputation had obviously preceded us. We found the dealership and were pleased to see a workshop behind it. After standing in the wrong section for a while we managed to obtain a set of brake pads. Continuing the extremely helpful theme of the Portuguese (perhaps this was the best country in the world after all), a mechanic approached us and ushered us into the workshop where he had a few Smarts on the ramps. He showed us the technique for changing the pads, which was very useful as one of the nuts we were convinced you had to remove, in fact, you couldn't – and shouldn't. Thanking him and armed with our bits we headed back to the track, using our detailed map. The pads, on both sides, were replaced. Again we were grateful to both Andrew and Paul (Mustang) and Steve and Frank (Mazda) for the loan of tools and jack.

'Let the brakes bed in a bit before you try any speed,' was the general advice from those in the know. The first bend, a right-hander, saw me pull the car round it at totally the wrong speed and in the wrong gear. The second bend was worse, and so on. Like a lot of things that look easy, once you start doing it, it proves to be a hell of a lot harder and within five minutes I couldn't believe how hot and sweaty I had become. The same thought occurred to me many many years ago after a drunken teenage party!

The final right-hand bend led us back onto the straight and gave us a chance to open up the Smart. We hurtled down the long straight before heavily braking into another right-hander, then another circuit of the track ensued with equally erratic driving. Finally we pulled into the pit lane. We were met with bemused looks. 'I thought you were going to bed the brakes in?'

'Yeah, I sort of forgot, mind you, they are now.' And with that, Adrian was off for a couple of laps before our tame racing driver could have a go.

We had tentatively booked Phiroze for the 1 p.m. slot and had panicked earlier when the brake problem arose. However, 1 p.m. arrived. As did Phiroze. The car was ready, but was Phiroze?

Phiroze asked me to take the driver's seat but I declined, asking him if he could drive so that I could see what the car was capable of doing. Having left the pit lane and moved smoothly onto the track and round the first couple of bends, Phiroze pointed out that he hadn't driven a Smart before; however his handling of the car was infinitely better than mine and the Smart eased its way round with two very surprised occupants as to its speed and handling. Like any good professional Phiroze made his chosen art seem so easy. We came down the straight at 100mph-plus, braked late and turned into a right-hander. Phiroze commented that the red Ferrari behind us (yes behind us) wasn't going to make the bend. I turned to see a cloud of shingle and stones and Carl's Ferrari ploughing through the undergrowth. If I had been driving I wouldn't have noticed my passenger, let alone what was going on behind me. Carl went off three times.

Adrian took a turn and it was nice to see the Smart speeding down the straight at Estoril and flying past us in the viewing area. Later we were informed that it hit 110mph on the straight. Phiroze left us and the car to drive another vehicle and we took it in turns to take the Smart round the track with our driving, times and positioning improving every lap. On one of the last laps I attempted, as a passenger, to dial a number on my mobile, in order to announce that we are doing 100mph on a racetrack at three-ish on a Tuesday afternoon, but the buffeting and momentum of the car was so great that I only managed to dial six or seven numbers without making a mistake. I gave up. Having 'hammered the hell out of the car' we headed off to Mérida in Spain, our checkpoint for the night.

12

Honey, Can We Go to Mérida Again?

The drive from the track to the centre of Mérida equated to 198 miles, which compared to the previous leg was just a walk in the park and coupled with the track day made the drive (which is the equivalent to London to Exeter) pass really quickly. Moving through the traffic on the outskirts of Lisbon the Smart coped really well and for the most part kept up with (and proved quicker than) a lot of the bigger cars. The traffic, thankfully, was flowing, and we found ourselves in no time passing over Lisbon's mini Golden Gate Bridge, the 25 de Abril Bridge. This was also the start of a run of wide, empty roads and the glorious sight of Paul and Stuart in their Corvette passing us at a speed for which a Corvette is designed.

We were approximately 100-odd miles further down the road, travelling at about 90–95mph when from behind us headlights appeared and within seconds were upon us, and past us. It was Carl and Steve in their Ferrari 430, which they were clearly pushing to the limit. The sight and sound of a Ferrari in full flight is a rarity in the UK, but not so in Europe. The uncrowded, good-quality roads allow cars to do what they are built for. This stretch also allowed for a near 200mph race between two of the other cars, and this was the main talking point. The cars had pushed themselves to the limit, their engines working overtime, so much so that even Kash's Lamborghini had produced so much heat from the engine that the rear number plate had warped and come unstuck from the body of the car. Now 'irresponsible', 'dangerous' and 'reckless' all spring to mind, and yes, could be argued for; however, taking the scenario of an M1 motorway in much better condition and completely empty for as far as the eye could see, was it so reckless? Our preconceived ideas, living as we do in this overpopulated country, are always shaped by our full and busy roads. The Cannonball type organisers, and Jan in particular, don't just pick a random 3,000 miles and say, 'Right let's just drive this.' No, a lot of hard work and 'trip running' beforehand takes place to find brilliant and safe roads, plus wonderful sights. Yes, we all speed, yes, the cars are exceptionally fast, but the type of person who takes their many thousands of pounds-worth of car on an event like this doesn't leave many things to chance.

Alcohol, that was the immediate next hurdle to cross and that night in Mérida proved to be one that encompassed everything about The Cannonball.

We had made good time and found ourselves on the outskirts of the fascinating town situated between Lisbon and Madrid. Mérida has the distinction of having more Roman monuments in better condition than anywhere else in Spain. Built in 24 BC it was originally called Emerta Augusta and later became known as Mérida, its name also being taken by two prominent towns in Venezuela and Mexico. Among its more famous buildings are the Roman theatre, which in its day could hold up to 6,000 in the audience plus the amphitheatre, capable of holding 15,000 spectators. The town also boasts the longest Roman bridge in Spain. We actually entered the town over a bridge called the 'Puente de Luisitania' that kindly saw us over the River Guadiana. Coming into the town we encountered a few one-way systems; however, even without the aid of sat nav we soon found the hotel for the night, a feat made slightly easier by the crescendo of high-performance cars parked outside, revving their engines, the sound of which echoed off the tight narrow lanes that led to the square and hotel. Plus of course, we were also following Ray and Graham in their BMW M3 complete with their sat nav.

Our hotel for the night, the Hotel Mérida Palace, was conveniently placed, overlooking the main square and offered distinguished previous guests including Queen Isabella II, her husband

Francisco De Asis, plus King Alfonso XII and now, almost 100 years later, Dave and Adrian from Essex driving a Smart car. The hotel was built in 1802 and had had some improvements carried out, one of the most noticeable being a bar on the ground floor. So, totally ignoring the splendid entrance hall, with its stunning mosaic designs, we grabbed a couple of San Miguels and adjourned to the patio to discuss another of Italy's finest, Carl and Steve's Ferrari 430 and the number of times it had left the track. Cars were arriving all the time and so were the spectators, with many locals turning up at the hotel, as word spread. The evening was ticking along quite well with drinks, more excited conversations and slightly more exaggerated stories about the track day, as the drink took effect, and then we headed off to a great open-air restaurant, being bussed there in two trips. It wasn't long before the drink was flowing, which I profusely apologised for, and accordingly offered to pay for any of the dry cleaning I was causing. I got chatting to Carl and rather refreshingly for him I didn't mention the track; however it transpired that we spent New Year's Eve in the same nightclub in Dubai. It proved to be yet another good night with a chance for all the drivers to meet, more so than the previous night for us, and the common theme of cars was shining through with a vast majority of cars in production seemingly owned or being owned by us all. It also appeared that at the track a couple of casualties were taken, namely Dean and Darren in their Vauxhall, which developed serious enough problems for them to leave it to be trailered home. They were going to continue, however, by hiring cars for the remainder of the trip. Sam and Colin's Vauxhall (spooky) also fell foul of the track, probably down to the tear-up with the mighty Smart, but I actually think it was an oil pump that caused the car's demise, and again they left the vehicle to be trailered back while they hitched lifts with accommodating other drivers.

The food was served and kept in theme with the open-air Roman theatre-style restaurant we were in. Having had an awful run of weather at home, the very mild night in Mérida was having a good effect on most of us and when time came to get the bus back to the hotel the vast majority of Cannonballers felt it was far too early to go to bed, and with a mild night plus a town square complete with bar and locals there was only one place to go.

One of the things I did pack in the Smart was six bottles of champagne plus plastic tumblers. Why? Well, the idea was to open a bottle each time we finished a leg and share it with the car that came in behind us. The first night we were last and the second night here in Mérida we just plain forgot, so what a Godsend when I remembered the bottles and headed off to the car accompanied by a few drivers and checkpoint girls. The cars were parked in the surrounding streets of the hotel and were obviously creating a stir among the locals, so when we got to the Smart there was a small throng of people hanging around. Not to appear inhospitable we offered champagne to them, including three 14-year-olds who seemed over the moon to get a drink, plus an assortment of zoom-zoomsmart T-shirts, stickers and badges. We left the now sozzled teenagers and carried the remaining bottles to the square where an impromptu party was now in full swing, including drivers, checkpoint girls, locals, the bar staff of the bar in the square, the local police, and a few American tourists who happened to be wandering past. The party went on and on, and to be fair the bar staff kept serving, so in true British fashion, we kept up our image of Brits abroad by drunkenly staggering round singing and spilling alcohol, while totally ignoring the beauty of the square and what would have been a tranquil night's sleep for the many travellers staying in Mérida. The American tourists had attempted to last the pace and were trying to inject some sort of sense into the proceedings; however they soon realised that us Brits aren't all like *Brideshead Revisited* or Stephen Fry. When trying to engage us in a conversation about the Roman Empire, for some reason all we could muster up was the fact that in our opinion, the Mafia had had its day along with their football team and the aqueducts were nothing without Jason! One American, John, had taken it upon himself to join in the numerous drinking games and drinking circles that had built up during the night and it proved to be a hilarious sight as he was dragged off home by his missus and her new Spanish 'friend' complete with the dragging-of-the-feet stance. I believe the new friend was kindly going to stay with 'Mrs John' while John was spark-out asleep to keep an eye on him. With that type of generosity and kind-heartedness, I think he must had some Portuguese in him and if so, no doubt Mrs John might benefit. The impromptu party ended about four-ish and we headed back to the hotel for a few hours' sleep before the next leg.

I woke expecting a hangover, but was slightly surprised to find hardly any side-effects from the copious amount of drink the night before. Adrian too was having no side-effects and we ventured downstairs for breakfast and a chat to anyone one who was there. The casualties from the previous night were growing, with numerous failures at the breathalyser test by the 'blow me boys', who every morning on the run wait, patiently, in some cases, for the drivers who have to pass the test before getting into the car. Adrian's Subaru was playing up again but given the fact that he was over the limit he had to wait in any case and carry out much needed repairs to the ailing beast. Having packed our bags and headed downstairs we set off to the car and packed the bags in the back, now with plenty of room having disposed of the champagne the previous night. Starting up the car and moving round the streets the obvious flaw in our plan had suddenly been realised. We didn't know where we were going.

'Barcelona bring it on'. Mission Pack Number 3 had been handed out and 593-mile journey was on – the equivalent of driving from London to just past Inverness. The A5 motorway was called upon, taking us directly to Madrid. We noticed the heat had progressively risen and was, indeed, welcome. The Smart moved off and across the Citra de Extremadura toward the A5. All of the chat in the car revolved around the previous night and before we knew it we were speeding along the A5 at a respectable 90mph. The Smart seemed to be enjoying the drive, running more smoothly and faster than previously, blessed with the now familiar smooth, open and empty roads. Chatting about the car, the thought of its top speed came up.

We had hit about 110mph on the track, but we had run out of straight, and with the lovely, lovely roads here in Spain surely we could beat that? As if the car was bugged or something the phone went. It was one of the checkpoint girls informing us to be on our guard as the Spanish police were out in force with reports coming in from other drivers that there was a big presence on the A5. The top speed attempt would have to wait. It wasn't long before we came across the first sighting of two police bikes and two cars on the side of the road; however they chose to ignore us just as I was getting Smarticus in Cadiz ready.

Driving on, the miles were diminishing as the temperature increased the closer we got to Madrid. Unlike the first leg, with its lack of sighting of other Cannonballers, this leg was proving different and we were slowly caught up and passed by Graham and Ray in their M3 BMW. The Smart was running extremely well; however, as the scenery was flat, bland, hot and dusty, our apathy level grew leading to the conversation in the car disappearing, with Adrian driving almost in an overdrive mentality. I found a packet of wine gums tucked away and excitedly grabbed them, only to find they had melted in the heat and were half congealed. We suddenly happened upon Graham and Ray who seemed to be explaining the mechanics of their car to a couple of policemen who had gone to the trouble of pulling them over for a chat. Brilliant! This revived both Adrian and myself and soon we were merrily chatting about their plight, and whether we would see them again, as this appeared to be bandit country and the police certainly seemed to have that hick town sheriff swagger about them.

Madrid was still a way to go however, and at this point a thorny issue was brought up. How would we get round (or through) Madrid in order to head for Barcelona? We could head down to Valencia on the coast and follow the coast round to Barcelona, but was that the best route? In the end we decided that we could tuck in behind one of the other Cannonballers with sat nav and follow them.

Pulling into a petrol station 20 miles from Madrid we struck lucky and bumped into Simon and Nick in their Z4M BMW. After filling up and following them out we headed towards Madrid which could clearly be seen, now, in the distance. One eye on Simon and Nick, the other on our trusted road map, I noticed a sign for Zaragoza which immediately rang bells with the football club, another place I had heard of in Spain; however, looking at the map I could see that we really should be heading for Zaragoza rather than following the ring road which, while taking you round Madrid, also takes you further into the capital and more traffic. A decision was taken and we pulled away from Simon and Nick and took the Zaragoza road, a decision confirmed as a good one when a sign for the airport appeared, reaffirming that we were on the right route as the airport is located on the correct side of Madrid in relation to where we wanted to go. We soon found the A2 to Zaragoza and, believe it or not, a sign for Barcelona! Hitting the A2 we slowed as the volume of traffic had built up and it dawned on us both that this was really the first time since leaving a rainy Sandown Park that we had got caught up in slow traffic on a main road. I took the chance to look around at Madrid's commuters and noticed that the Smart was causing a great deal of interest among the other drivers, and a few waves and smiles were exchanged before the traffic began to clear. Very soon we were off again on clear uncluttered roads, averaging 85–90mph with the occasional burst to 100-plus. I took over the reins and settled in for the final run to Barcelona. The car was running hot, and we only really appreciated why when getting some petrol. The outside temperature was stifling and we were back to the very barren landscapes. The journey was therefore lacking in things to do other than point the car and drive it, which is what we did.

Passing through the wasteland I was amazed at the similarity between what I was seeing and that of Arizona and the wide-open spaces of New Mexico. The heat too was very similar plus the nice long empty roads, and due to this at last we made Zaragoza in good time, skirting round to continue on to Barcelona. Between Zaragoza and Barcelona the scenery changes a little bit with more hills and a little greenery thrown in. The hilly, windy roads proved good fun with the chance to use all three lanes in places, cutting corners and buzzing local drivers. 'Buzzing' basically involved seeing a car in the distance and accelerating towards it, passing as close as possible and therefore maximising the effect of the speed we were doing, something admittedly very juvenile and better effected by two or three cars in tandem, not a lonely Smart in the middle of Spain. Nevertheless it made me laugh, well chuckle, well, all right, it wasn't funny at all and really was only done to liven up the journey a bit.

As the journey continued the heat rose, the roads cleared even more, and a sort of cruise control took over in my head. It was lucky therefore that a blur of a sign went past and then a bigger sign, proudly proclaiming that we had just passed the Greenwich meridian line! The journey was broken up again when a Volkswagen bus with British number plates was spotted and we slowed to take in the view of a couple of bohemian occupants driving a classic and at a very respectable speed, probably taking months to cover the same distance we were doing in five days.

The last town we passed before Barcelona was Lleida, about an hour outside Barcelona. The town was hosting some sort of graffiti championship with 'artists' and fans coming from all around the world. Perhaps that was where our bohemian friends were heading, although they had looked more in favour of a guitar and a beach. We pushed on to Barcelona, finally reaching the last toll before the city.

13

Ooh Look, We're on Television

'Look, there's a police escort for us into town,' said Adrian, and I glanced across to the right of the tolls and saw a few blue and red flashing lights with eight or so Cannonballers lined up behind them.

'Wouldn't get that at home,' I said, now trying to manoeuvre the car across six lanes to the right-hand side toll to join the procession. 'We've done really well, there only appear to be eight cars ahead of us,' I carried on as I headed for the convoy.

Adrian, proving to be more attentive than me, suddenly pointed out that the police seemed to be taking quite an interest in the cars, in fact too much interest. Now if you have ever tried to look inconspicuous, don't try it in a Union Jack adorned Smart car, in a traffic jam, at a toll, in Spain, while trying to make your way back across six lanes of traffic. Horns started, accompanied by shouting, and numerous gesticulations. Adrian and I tried to put on that 'distant' look as if we did this all the time and had nothing to do with those rascals in their Ferraris and Astons. It seemed to work as while the police had definitely spotted us, along with every other car inhabitant that side of the tolls, we must have looked too disorganised and comical to be in the same league as the British supercar street racers. The police let us pass. In fact I swear that some of them even turned their glances away from us in sheer embarrassment.

Ah, the road to Barcelona and our hotel, the Gran Hotel Princess Sofia, situated really close to the Nu Camp and dead simple to find! We followed the dual carriageway that takes you into the city centre with a view to coming off after a couple of kilometres to join the Autopista B23, which in turn joins up with the

Avinguda Diagonal, off which our hotel was situated. The first part went swimmingly well. Then the phone went. It was Jan from The Cannonball telling us to be on our guard as the police were out and a lot of cars were being pulled. We told her that we had seen the roadblock at the tolls but had 'stealthily moved round it'.

We found ourselves on the B23, excellent; at last we were getting the hang of directions, and so on to the Diagonal. In principle the roads just sort of merge, however they merge not just with themselves but with the C32 *and* the B20, along with a couple of smaller roads. Without sat nav and a detailed map of Barcelona we found ourselves on the B20, believing it to be the correct road. It wasn't long before we started to see signs that weren't in keeping with where we wanted to go and doubts crept in, especially when one of the signs mentioned 'Montpellier' being 340km. A decision had to be made as to whether to continue to the next main junction and do a U-turn or come off at the next immediate junction and try to make our way through the back streets back to our hotel. The latter was decided on and the next junction taken. The Avinguda Diagonal is a main road and serves numerous larger roads, making it easy to find, but not for us. We continued zig-zagging across Barcelona with some places looking familiar, but only because we had passed them numerous times in the past hour. Finally, we stumbled upon Avinguda Meridiana, a road that actually appeared on our map, but where were we in relation to everything else? With a toss of a euro we turned left and travelled along with the traffic. The euro had been kind to us and we came upon a large junction-come-roundabout. Behold, on the opposite side we spied the hotel, which, of course, we couldn't pull into from our side of the road. This necessitated a further five minutes' travelling in the wrong direction before we could turn round. Finding ourselves on the right side of the road *and* on the right road in the right city, we pulled up at the hotel via a bus lane, causing a local bus driver to get annoyed about something. Maybe it was the handful of passengers slamming against the front window of the bus as he put his airbrakes to the test rather than hitting a Union Jack-emblazoned Smart car.

The Princesa Sofia is an imposing hotel situated close to the Camp Nu, Barcelona football club's ground, in the heart of the financial district. The hotel has a nice bar where we relaxed having checked in and dumped our bags on our beds. The stories of the day mainly centred around the tolls and the police roadblock. As more and more drivers arrived, it was apparent that the cars held were in for a long haul. Dean and Darren turned up in a rather ill-running hire car which apparently had blown a gasket or something, testament to the driving skills and terminal speed they were trying to get out of the car. They were to return this car and be forced to source a car on the French-Spanish border as they were prohibited from taking a hire car from one country to another. We left them to sort this out while I wrestled with the conundrum of carrying three pints of lager and two dishes of nuts from one end of the bar to the other. After chatting and drinking for a while the first of the cars arrived from the tolls and it wasn't long, thankfully, before they all came in. It seemed that the police were waving them over once they had passed the toll. Rumour had it that the tickets given in at the toll showing the time at the previous toll were a clear indication of the speed they had done from one toll to another: they must have been speeding. The police were pulling in cars with British number plates apart from, it would seem, the two clowns in the Smart car, and explaining that they were in a rally, which was illegal in Spain. The main giveaway was in fact not the registration plates but the stamp on all our hands confirming that we had been passed by the blow me boys, that morning, leading to vehement denials of being part of The Cannonball, quickly dampened with a 'Please roll up your sleeve,' to reveal the stamp. One pair who had lost their stamps through natural sweat were Kevin and Robbie, who also lost pounds, almost stones! Their TVR decided to be a normal TVR and show signs of resentment at being driven. The electrics were having their own fun and to combat the car over-heating the heater had to be on full blast with the windows refusing to budge as they travelled through the middle of Spain in 90-odd degrees. The underground car park of the hotel was stage for the

TVR to then decide to release the hold on the windows with them coming down and going up, while the indicators decided to flash away and window wipers came into action, all while we stood a few feet from the car and even a fewer feet more from Kevin and Robbie as the unattended TVR did its floor show for us. Not content with the electrics stealing the show, the bonnet of the car decided to get in on the act and became impossible to hold down without reams of gaffer tape. Whilst the cars were coming in to the hotel and drivers relaxing, word spread of a TV extravaganza on one or two of the news channels covering the cars and drivers being held on the side of the road.

Washed, showered and ready to go, we boarded the coach for the exclusive Opium Mar restaurant and bar, situated next to the famous Arts Hotel and on the beach. The coach pulled up and a good deal of 'fired-up Cannonballers' literally jumped off to get to the bar. Food was served, again excellent, as was the company at our table (well I was sitting there wasn't I?). We were joined at the restaurant by one of last year's drivers, a complete lunatic called Stevie who had flown from Scotland to Barcelona just for the night and, despite numerous requests to continue on for the next few days, returned back to Edinburgh in the morning. Coupled with Stevie's enthusiasm and the already fired-up Ballers, when the nearby club opened, it was hit with a force of drunk over-enthusiastic drivers showing the first-arrival clubbers a few shapes and moves, plus how to scull bottles of San Miguel in record time. The club began to fill up, with our VIP section getting larger and larger as we took advantage of the young, vibrant Barcelona clubbers, alcohol, and our Cannonball reputation which was growing throughout the night with a lot of tourists and British expats treating us like celebrities and rather recklessly buying us drinks. A few of us were questioned about the 'incident' earlier which was shown more and more on Spanish television and by the time the drinks had kicked in the story became more and more stretched. Daniel from the Audi RS6, however, was impressed with the fact that at about 140mph they had hit a bird which careered off their windscreen leaving its skin of sorts welded to it. Invariably I would be asked what car I was in. Even pissed, your conscience pricks you – do you lie and boast a Ferrari or Aston? Or smile inanely and say 'Smart car'? I chose the honest answer and found myself having to convince people I wasn't actually in an Aston or similar.

A really strange phenomenon then happened. The club was buzzing, the music was good, people were nice, but we still wanted to leave and find somewhere else. A few of us did so, taking cabs to all four corners of the city, a lot of us heading to La Rambla and the numerous bars there. More bars, more drink, ensued with further cab journeys before, knackered, we made it back to the hotel to find a ragged bunch of drunk drivers wandering around the foyer trying to either find their rooms or more bars. The one thing that became obvious that night was the fact that we were staying in high-quality hotels in really interesting places but seeing none of the cities nor hotels really.

After what seemed like seconds after shutting the hotel room door and getting into bed the thorny issue of breakfast arose. Sleep, all four hours, passed really quickly and we were back up, getting ready for the 10 a.m. meeting, except the 10 a.m. meeting was encouraged to be earlier due to heavy pressure from the police for us to get, not only out of Barcelona, but of Spain. A hurried cooked breakfast was had and the blow me boys called into action. At least 50 per cent of the drivers passed, therefore enabling us to get all the cars out of the underground car park and on the road. One of those moments when you think 'Is this really happening?' took place at the morning briefing. Dean of Dean and Claire fame came down dressed as Batman, obviously to help us fight of the police. I didn't know whether Bruce and Craig had pulled the night before, going out dressed in Arabic national dress but Dean was suddenly engulfed by about a dozen or so Arabic-looking people who all wanted their photo taken with him, all this going on with the serious backdrop of Jan and the organisers trying to tell us the best way to deal with the police and a strong media presence outside the hotel, plus Irish Dave from the BMW giving a very hungover press conference to all and sundry while a photo frenzy was being carried out in the foyer with Batman and all these Arabs.

Coming out of the car park we were in fact met by the police and TV cameras, a bit like following West Ham a few years ago! We headed past them to join the Avinguda and the road out of town.

Adrian and I managed to take all the right roads, admittedly a lot of them looking familiar from the day before, to get out of Barcelona and on the road to Perpignan and onward to the next destination – Vichy.

Vichy is 427 miles from Barcelona, the equivalent of driving from London to just past Glasgow. It is situated north of Lyon just above the Massif Central, therefore taking us through some lovely scenic routes. It is famous for being a spa town and came into being in 52 BC, being established by the Romans. Benefiting from thermal baths, in 1799 Laetitia Bonaparte took her less famous son Louis to Vichy to be cured of an illness, leaving Napoleon home alone. More importantly, in my eyes, about 150 years before Mrs B turned up, the House of Bourbon was set up here, and I'm not talking about the biscuits.

Back to the main road out of Barcelona, then, and the Smart was again running well, cutting in and out of the commuter traffic and heading hopefully for sanctuary and the French border. Not content with ruining our breakfast, the Spanish police had decided to post cars and officers along the side of the roads and had a helicopter monitoring us. Leaving the confines of Barcelona and well on our way to Perpignan the police presence died down and we were free to pick up the pace again which the Smart did. Now I don't know whether it was the track day, the long, hot journey through Spain, or the fact we were actually heading in the right direction for home, but for the first time on the whole trip I became interested in times, and more importantly the fact that the Smart wasn't going to end up languishing in the lower positions, which I honestly felt it didn't deserve. France was approaching and the tolls, but more worryingly was the fact that the traffic was building up. Why? Were the French police planning something for us? We decided after consulting our map that we could leave the motorway at the next junction and pass through the little towns running parallel with the motorway, thereby avoiding the tolls and any police roadblock we had convinced ourselves would be waiting. All worked really well as we travelled through truck-stop type towns with all types staring at us and in some cases chasing the car on foot. Deciding that perhaps being banged up with 'bubba' wouldn't be that bad compared to what we were driving through, we rejoined the motorway about five miles from the toll to find the traffic moving freely, meaning that there obviously wasn't a roadblock or that there was and we had missed it. The toll was upon us and we found ourselves behind a Spanish 1975 911s Porsche coupe which had been converted for rallies. As it accelerated away the sound from the exhaust was impressive, although when we had paid our fee we found ourselves not too far behind and had an enjoyable ten miles following the car, listening to it accelerate and crackle and pop as it slowed down. The subject of the Smart and the timings came back and with Adrian's superior mathematical brain, to me that is, he set about attempting to calculate some times we would have to do in order to get close to the magical 61mph.

Our route to Vichy would take us past Perpignan on the A75 toward Montpellier, following the A75 to Clermont-Ferrand and then on to Vichy. Adrian calculated that if we did it in seven hours exactly we would bring our time close enough to 61 for the next and last day. I drove that day, and it was also the day that we decided, if given the chance, to see what the Smart could do. Perpignan came and went and on we pushed to Montpellier, taking in the sights and phone calls received in the car to the extent that unfortunately, I missed the turn-off for the A75 and was only five miles from Montpellier before Adrian noticed. This was just as well as I would have merrily driven right into the heart of the city. After stopping to consult the map it was decided to take the back roads for Saint Saturnin. The B road taking us there was the worst scenario for us. It seemed the majority of the road was undergoing improvement, therefore making it a single lane with a lot of traffic.

Could we patiently wait in line? NO! When the opportunity arose we decided to take it and like a professional slalom skier elegantly flowing down the side of a mountain, the Union Jack-emblazoned Smart slipped in and out of the gaps kindly left by the locals, narrowly missing the cars and lorries coming in the opposite direction. This style of driving bought us some good time and we found ourselves back on the A75 and the smooth clear dual carriageway where the car picked up speed again. The scenery was beginning to change, becoming more hilly and mountainous, with the road winding up and then down again. Picking up speed all the time the Smart was taking everything in its stride: the hills, the inclines, the bends, and passing most things on the road. Now I'm not a religious man; however, on a gradual incline which was becoming more steep with more and more sharp bends, I was shocked to see a vehicle closing in rapidly. I put my foot down a bit more, getting the wheels to squeal their displeasure each time we took a bend, but the vehicle was still closing. It caught us and passed by, pushing on, taking the bends and hills in its stride. It was a white Citroën van that didn't seem to flinch at the bends nor break its stride. Adrian, never one to miss an opportunity, suggested that next year we could do The Cannonball in one.

This wasn't the end of the white Citroën van in our adventures: the Lord would provide one again. Petrol calling, we pulled in at a service station and filled up. The air seemed very fresh, testament to the area and height we were at, plus the heat was still with us. Getting settled we pulled off and made our way to the main road from the service station, when just in front of us two girls in their early twenties appeared with rucksacks and a healthy bronzed complexion which became visible after they proceeded to take their jackets off, leaving skimpy tops and jeans. One of them stuck her thumb out in that universal way of obtaining a lift. A summer of love travelling round Europe beckoned and passed just as quickly; there was just not enough room in the Smart – mind you what a book that could have been!

Now thoroughly depressed and back on the road we had to

cheer ourselves up and so it was time to test the Smart, as the roads had cleared of traffic and appeared to be less hilly. Pushing the car harder we were getting to between 110 and 115mph but then a bend would loom and we were forced to slow. This went on for some time, becoming more and more frustrating as the Smart still had some more left in it. The roads were now looking familiar again, with inclines and bends, so the attempt would have to wait. Aimlessly driving along admiring the view, discussing the speed attempt and where we would be now if we had a four-seater or a camper van, we turned a corner to be absolutely gobsmacked.

The Millau Bridge is awe-inspiring. Opened in December 2004 after about three years in the building, the Michel Virlogeux and Norman Foster design boasts the tallest vehicular bridge in the world. At its height it is taller than the Eiffel Tower and a mere 125ft shorter than the Empire State Building. Mind you, this was not the first time that we came across Michel Virlogeux; oh no, he actually had a major influence in the building of the Vasco da Gama Bridge we crossed in Lisbon.

The site as we came upon it certainly slowed us down as we took in the stunning view. The crossing again encapsulated the work that obviously went into that year's route: not only were we staying in lovely hotels and visiting brilliant clubs and restaurants, our journeys were also taking in some very special sights. Paying our toll after crossing we utilised the A75 to push on to Vichy. Behold! A sight that we had been waiting for: an empty road that stretched as far as we could see. The speed attempt was on.

'Brace yourself,' I said as I began to crank the little Smart up, and up she went: 85, 90, 95 . . . 'How we doing?'

'Fine, loads of road left,' said Adrian.

'Quick, get the camera ready.' I kept the car to 100mph so that Adrian could 'get the camera ready'. Pushing my foot down still further the car was still responding, albeit a little slower, and the speedo edged up: 115mph, 'Ready?', 117mph, 'Ready?', *Click*.

'What you doing?' I said.

'Taking the photo,' said Adrian, leaning across me at 117mph.

'No, leave it, I can get more.' *Click.* 'Not yet!'

'We're running out of road again,' Adrian said in a casual voice but showing signs of early panic.

'No, a little bit more!' I tried to force my foot through the body-work of the car. Approximately 122–124mph was recorded and I shouted to Adrian, ' Look, look! Get a picture!'

All Adrian could do while trying to lean across me was to mention that the road had virtually run out. I braked hard. *Click.* 'What the fuck was that for?'

'To get a picture,' he obviously replied. While it appeared that we had slowed dramatically, that last photo still recorded 100mph. The best photo we got was at 115mph. The whole speed test was done with two adults and luggage, and we definitely got the needle off the dial.

Slowing dramatically and now ambling along at 80–85mph, we calculated we had about two and a half hours until Vichy and the issue of where the hotel might be and how big was Vichy? Our relative peace was suddenly interrupted by a familiar sound: the yellow mustang of Mike and Andrew came alongside and as it cruised past we pulled out behind it. Travelling along at 90-odd miles an hour we stuck to the second lane. I had put my window down and was listening to their throbbing V8 engine, which sounded fantastic. At this point life was spot on. The scenery in this part of the world is really nice and from the A75 you could see lovely small French towns passing you below or in the distance. The weather was warm and bright and all this to the accompaniment of a 500-plus bhp Mustang. Now, hovering between 95 and 100mph (so much for slowing down), we came upon and passed Philip and Lisa in their Lotus Elise who joined us, forming a three-car convoy. The remaining two hours to Vichy proved to be very enjoyable with the three of us swapping positions and at one stage passing round the sweets at 80mph from car to car. Plus, of course, we again had an escort which meant we would find the hotel with ease.

Again the hotel didn't disappoint. The Sofitel Les Celestins was a lovely four-star hotel with stunning views over Lake Allier. Even more impressive was the bar that greeted us after checking in the car and then checking in ourselves. The now normal practice of going to our room, throwing down the bags and heading back downstairs for a swift one was again religiously followed and in record time, Adrian and myself found ourselves at the bar with Adrian (Subaru) and Daniel the bird-killer (RS6). I decided that I would have a red wine rather than the obligatory beer which went down really quickly as would a beer, so another was ordered closely followed by another.

Meanwhile, the Smart had been booked in for a valet and my car keys were taken to move the car. A couple of wines later an anxious-looking youngster and one of the checkpoint girls came to our table and asked whose was the Mini? The car had self-locked with the keys inside. After a few wines it's the sort of thing that you do find quite funny which we did, but still managed to sympathise with the very nervous-looking car valeter. Five minutes or so later he was back, having located Jon and Greig who owned the Mini and got a spare set of keys. His state of euphoria rapidly turned to depression again when it dawned on him that a Smart isn't a Mini and a Mini isn't a Smart. His depression was compounded even more when he asked who owned the Smart car and was pointed to the person who was attempting the 'as many glasses of wine in an hour record'. Almost crying, he approached our table and gave us the good news that the car had been cleaned but the keys were locked inside. Having found the incident earlier quite funny it would have been hypocritical of me to get all stressed about it: well, in fact, after the wine I had drunk it would have been impossible for me to get at all stressed, so as casual as one could be after sculling almost a bottle of red in about an hour, we headed out to the very clean car. Like surgeons standing over an operating table Adrian and myself casually asked for the valet's buffing glove, which was produced, a hanger or piece of wire, which was produced, and a screwdriver, which was produced. The keys had been left on the driver's seat which made the job of retrieving them a lot easier than if they had been in the ignition. In no time at all we prized the widow open, filled the gap with the glove, slipped the wire in and hooked up the keys, much to the relief of the valet. To celebrate the fact that the keys were returned, I think you can now see where this is going; we had another couple of wines, finally heading for dinner at the award-winning restaurant on the side of the lake. The food was excellent and was accompanied by wine. Fuelled with wine my thoughts returned to earlier that day and the magical drive behind the Mustang with the Smart keeping pace at 100mph for most of it. Sitting quietly for a few moments the preceding days and, in particular, the car and how it had performed, made me even more determined for it not to finish way down the list. A full glass of red plonked onto the table bought me out of my thoughts and to matters at hand. Like a lot of places in the middle of France, while having a plethora of cafés and restaurants, nightclubs seemed to be a bit thin on the ground. Stimulated by red wine I and a few others were hell-bent on pushing on. The checkpoint girls were called upon to enquire about clubs. One imaginatively called 'Le Vichy Club' was the only place open, and approximately ten minutes' walk from the hotel, so it was with a spring in our steps, a few of mine were actually straight, that about a dozen of us headed over there.

The entrance was a small door with a bouncer, of types, and having, rather easily, negotiated a reduced entrance fee we went in. Immediately we could see why a reduced fee was agreed, because we doubled the crowd in there; however, desperate for drinks, we headed, I would have loved to have said pushed our way, but that really wasn't necessary, to the bar. The night went on and it became apparent that the 1970s hadn't really died that night in Vichy, with an assortment of music, clothes, people, décor complete with glitterball, and cheesy DJ phrases making the place the perfect time-warp and yes that classic from *The Rocky Horror Show* was played. The music played on and the drinks carried on, culminating in very drunk dancing with very drunk locals. Making our way back to the hotel it dawned on me that tomorrow was the last day and that strangely enough, a lot of people who weren't too concerned where they finished the race, had gone missing earlier in the night. One little anecdote from that night, so the story goes, was that one of our esteemed racing driver types had taken a shine to one of our lovely checkpoint girls. Armed with a bottle of France's finest bubbly and a duplicate key while us 70s rejects were doing our thing for Vichy's elite night people, he stealthily climbed the stairs and carefully let himself into the unsuspecting girl's room. Just about to deliver a crushing one-liner and pop his cork, imagine his surprise when he found the object of his affections already entertaining a fellow driver!

14

120mph Without a Hitch(hiker)

Morning came and up for breakfast, no real anticipation today of our destination as obviously it was north and ultimately Brighton and the Grand Hotel on the seafront. What sort of day would it be, this last of our adventure?

Rain and a slight drizzle is what greeted us as we left the hotel to fetch the car, not really ideal conditions to blast to Calais and the Channel Tunnel. Having collected Mission Pack Number 5, 'Ballers to Brighton', the 433 miles, the equivalent of driving from London to Manchester and back, commenced and within a mile we pulled into a petrol station and filled up. Excited chatter filled the fore-court as cars were coming in and out, all from The Cannonball, and this being the last day the atmosphere seemed more charged and determined. In order to reach a respectable average time, Adrian had calculated that we had to average 69.71mph, therefore having to complete the journey in six hours and 21 minutes, all well and good but the route looked liked it would take us through Paris!

Heading onto the A71 the rain was getting slightly heavier; however, we took the Smart up to 70mph, slowly increasing the speed where and when we could. The traffic on the dual carriage-way was fairly light to start with, but as we headed further north and into the more built-up areas it got heavier. The French roads are particularly good at showing the locations of petrol and service stations, and if we were to get anywhere near a respectable time the Smart's petrol consumption would have to be used to its best, therefore, planning the petrol stops would be paramount. Orleans was the first big city we would pass, 177 miles from Vichy and with a full tank of petrol this was easily achievable. The rain persisted, constantly dumping heavier falls and then reverting back to drizzle. The inside carriageway was again being dominated by lorries and now the ubiquitous caravans – yes, it was that time and they seemed to be out with a vengeance. It was the first time that we were both conscious of the time restraint hanging over us and with this firmly on our minds, the agonising delay each time one of the lumbering beasts slipped out of the slow lane to overtake another of the inhabitants, was showing itself as we started to push harder. The rain now falling more heavily and a mixture of spray and rain was hampering our chances. The sheer safety aspect was also beginning to play on our minds.

Our aim had been to get to the Paris outskirts by 1 p.m. and even in these conditions this still seemed possible. The Smart also seemed to sense the urgency and again the little car was responding brilliantly, not missing a beat as we, every now and then, pushed for a burst of speed to get away from potential hold-ups. The defining moment of the last day came just outside Orleans. Three Cannon-ballers went past us as we were caught on the inside lane, supercars all three. Two of them pulled off into a petrol station leaving one which we tucked in behind. Keeping to an average of 80mph we sensed with the weather conditions that the driver of the car wasn't enjoying things very much as there was a certain amount of erratic breaking and a reluctance to go over 80mph. This was confirmed a couple of miles past Orleans; he indicated to pull into the slow lane, clearly backing off on the speed. I instinctively put my foot down and all three of us responded – yes I am referring to the Smart here – we were on! The Smart smoothly moved up to the 95–100mph mark and as the rain came down, the music went up and Paris approached. The carriageway known as the A10 took us to the outskirts of Paris where the idea was to try and skirt round the city and head for Lille, then ultimately on to Calais and the finish. Petrol was also becoming a factor. Should we push on past Paris and fill up for the final push, or bite the bullet and fill up *this* side of

Paris and run the risk of stopping again? Each petrol stop wastes approximately 10 to 15 minutes, by the time you slow down to pull in, fill up and pay for the petrol, get on the road again and back up to average speed, and now with time very much at the forefront of our thoughts, could we spare the time? On the other hand if the traffic proved to be heavy in and around Paris we might actually run out of fuel and be completely knocked off the rankings. The decision was made to pull in and fill up at the next station, also due to the fact that the previous night's excesses were starting to play havoc with my stomach.

Screaming into the service station I was half out the car before it had stopped and was running for the toilet while Adrian parked the car, having moved over, and started to fill it with petrol. I thankfully made it to where I was going and decided on the way out to grab some water and provisions. I bumped into Derek from one of the Ferrari 430s who told me that Will, his co-driver, was suffering like me. Derek and Will had apparently dined out last night in one of Vichy's restaurants. Adrian pulled up outside the shop and I was in the car in seconds. He then promptly got out and decided he needed to relieve himself also, thankfully in the WC. Sitting in the car waiting for him I noticed a few glances from fellow road-users and soon the car was attracting a lot of attention, with fellow Brits engaging me in conversations about the car and The Cannonball. Adrian came out and had to squeeze past a few of our newly-found fans, and with this we made our excuses and headed off. A few hundred yards down the road I stopped and reversed up to the 'fans': I had managed to find a few badges and stickers left in the car and handed these out. Leaving again to a great cheer we set off, only for me to stop a second time to hand a family of four who were heading to their car the last of the stickers and badges. They looked a bit bemused by the whole thing and thanked me: in Dutch.

Back on the road again and we were soon on the E15 and beginning the swoop of Paris. Rather alarmingly, the traffic heading in the opposite direction was proving to be quite heavy and we felt sure that it wouldn't be long before our direction would suffer.

Pushing on now, zig-zagging in between the traffic, we used the Smart to its best by creating lanes between lanes, ignoring the fact that there was a very thin hard shoulder by cutting down it more than once. Given that the car was festooned with a Union Jack and being driven in a way that would probably undo all the good work of the *Entente Cordiale*, we probably only got away with it because we were so blatant with our bad driving that the other drivers must have thought a film was being made.

There was still no real sign of traffic apart from a few hold-ups and then the Smart became a bike and shot down the hard shoulder. We were making good time. Signs for Lille were now being spotted and our spirits lifted even more, if that was possible, with all the excitement of the drive we were currently undertaking. Taking the Lille junction, narrowly missing a couple of cars which had the temerity to be between us and the turn-off, we pushed on and had our first glimpse of a real sign, one showing Lille, Brussels and Calais. Good news! We had obviously got our directions right plus we were on the right side of Paris! We picked up the A1, the final piece of this automobile jigsaw, and headed to Calais.

As we neared Calais I was conscious of the French police lying in wait to catch speeding motorists who were late for the ferries and trains to the UK, so I mentally made sure to stick to 80mph, the speed limit, the closer we got to Calais. However, Adrian informed me that while we were making good time, 80mph probably wouldn't be enough, so the dilemma of a very good time or just a good time would fall on fate or how awake the local police were. I felt safe enough, if it ever was safe, to ask of the Smart another 100mph burst and even after 2,800 miles it responded brilliantly. A new buzz was now beginning to kick in as, firstly, for every minute we were getting closer to the end, a bit like you must be feeling reading this book, and secondly, we were now beginning to see a lot more British cars and passing them at over 100mph with the knowledge of what we had just done over the previous five days giving a great feeling of just downright rebellion. Adrian was now consulting the calculator on my phone, working down the miles and letting me know what speeds we should be doing. We would still have to do over 80mph the closer we got to Calais.

Arras was upon us, home to the footballing dynasty the Benoit Assou-Ekottos, who play for Tottenham and RE Mouscron in Belgium. That was about all Arras had to interest us, and to be fair even if it had the two lovely, lovely hitchhikers from the Pyrenees that we passed earlier the previous day, I doubt we would have stopped, so intent now were we on finishing. The issue of speed still slightly worried us, because to make a very good time would mean travelling at a faster speed than the police would allow and we were now certainly entering bandit country. Hovering around the 85mph mark we were passed by a white Citroën van – no, not the one from before but very similar, who was doing around the 100mph mark. Being French and speeding and large, it proved to be the perfect foil for us, and without further ado we pulled out behind it and hooked in a few feet from its back bumper. The rationale behind this act was that firstly it could shield us from any speed traps, secondly it was local and probably knew where any police hotspots would be, and thirdly it was doing almost 100mph, perfect for getting our average up. The three-lane motorway to Calais was running well with no hold-ups and our friend was doing a great job overtaking everything in sight, moving from the third lane to the first with a Smart car inches from his bumper. We started to laugh as the driver of the van would pull out from the first lane to overtake, as would we, seconds later, and pull back again, as would we. We had the impression that he thought he was in a race with us and to confirm this he pushed on, picking up speed all the time and pleasing us no end.

We turned from the A1 to the A26 with now about 70 miles to go and thankfully so did our friend. Adrian was still working out the time-to-distance ratio and with the van driver's help we were on course to do a good time, still averaging 90–95mph. We were passing quite a few British cars and getting flashed by a few of them. Whether this was due to the speed we were doing or the novelty of a Union Jack Smart car I don't know, but every flash of headlights seemed to add to the excitement of the whole thing.

Disaster struck just before St Omer and about 40 miles from Calais when the white van pulled off the A road, presumably for St Omer, and we were left to travel solo. Adrian had confirmed that we were on course if we kept to 80mph but with the earlier speed bursts the petrol was looking dodgy. We were again faced with the old conundrum: if we pulled in it would add time, so should we risk it and hopefully make it to the port and worry about petrol the other side? The decision was made to push on with the luxury of dropping to 75mph, well within the speed limit. The last few miles were a countdown: we had 12 minutes to do them in and hopefully that would give us a good average speed. Closing in on Calais we saw one of the Cannonballers sitting on the side of the road, obviously having arrived too early. The remaining two miles saw us following Philip and Lisa in the Lotus, the car we set off behind that morning, but even stranger we were going to finish The Cannonball right behind the car we parked next to six days earlier at the hotel in Weybridge.

Turning into the Channel Tunnel terminal we saw The Cannonball checkpoint and Adrian claimed we were two minutes early!

'Stop and wait here,' he said, but I didn't want to, saying that it would look a bit crap to come all this way and then sit and wait. So we compromised and let the car crawl to the finish line, barely travelling over 3mph. We finally crossed the line with Adrian pushing the car. Checked in, we drove over to meet up with the ten or so cars that were already there and pulled up with them in readiness for the crossing and a leisurely drive to Brighton. Excited chatter filled the air with various claims of winning and how well people had done, but the overriding chat was about the event itself and what an experience it had been.

We boarded the train and parked up for the half-hour journey back before hitting the UK shores and the short trip from Ashford to Brighton: 81 miles, which is the equivalent of driving from say Ashford to Brighton. We pulled off the train and straight into the nearest petrol station to fill up and wait for the 11 cars that made

the first crossing, in order that we could travel in convoy to the
Grand Hotel. Immediately on hitting the M20 we were struck with
the unevenness and bumpiness of the road, really noticeable compared to the 2,900 smooth miles recently travelled in Europe. The
roads, particularly M20, were quite frankly rubbish in quality and
it was commented upon by all the drivers, the marked difference
between the volume of traffic and the standard of roads compared
to the three countries we had been through. So we bumped and
stopped and bumped and stopped all the way to Brighton in our
11-car convoy, finally arriving and slowly passing along the seafront,
past the pier and a sporadic rag-tag bunch of tourists and locals
who seemed to be drawn to the candy floss and doughnuts that are
plentiful in that area. Moving onto the hotel forecourt we pulled up
and were welcomed by the ever-present checkpoint girls and a glass
of champagne.

So that was it: the 2008 Cannonball Run over and the Smart car
looking proud as punch sitting amongst the first cars to arrive at
the Grand. Unpacking the car and checking in, we headed up to our
room, this time slowly unpacking and then wandering downstairs to
the bar. We met Dean and Claire from the Honda, Dean of Batman
fame, and spent an enjoyable time chatting and reminiscing about
the previous five days, gradually being joined by other drivers. A bit
merry, it was time to go back to the room and get changed into our
dinner suits for the grand final ball.

Back downstairs and back to the bar for a champagne-fest.
General excitable chat filled the room, a mixture of both the champagne kicking in and the release of adrenaline having completed
The Cannonball. A short film of The Cannonball was being shown
and I couldn't help noticing a cheer every time the Smart appeared
on the screen. We were all called to our respective tables to sit down
and again the film was shown, a short 15 minutes of our 3,000-mile
odyssey. Dinner was served and what the hotel was lacking compared to its European counterparts it made up in the food department, offering a fine evening which kept everyone happy.

Jan stood up and took the microphone to address us. She relayed some of the events and thanked the hardworking checkpoint girls, blow me boys, and photographers and cameramen. Then came the all-important announcement: who had won? And who had the Spirit of the Cannonball? In true tradition the results were announced in reverse order.

To the soundtrack of 'Mustang Sally': 'In third place, Andrew and Michael in the Mustang!' A great cheer went up, and up they went to collect their trophy.

To the soundtrack of 'I Drove All Night': 'In second place, Jamie and Anisa in the BMW!' Again a cheer went up, and up they went to collect their trophy. And finally, first place . . .

I had enjoyed the whole thing and was sitting at the table in a slightly merry state, congratulating myself on working out the link between Roy Orbison, 'I Drove All Night' and Jamie and Anisa: obviously it related to the first night when they powered through France, Spain and Portugal. I spied my wine glass nearly empty, closely followed by 'result' as I noticed a nearly full bottle of red cowering near the middle of the table. I reached out to get it.

'. . . and Adrian in the Smart car,' interrupted my chain of thought, closely followed by a huge cheer. Adrian jumped up and I followed, suddenly charged with 1,000 volts of energy. We won! I honestly couldn't believe it, but what eclipsed the first rush of winning was the genuine feeling of congratulations coming from everyone in the room, something to this day I will never forget. Adrian and I went up and collected our large trophies and again milked every drop of the adulation and applause, before returning to our seats and being accosted by Andrew from the Mustang, pointing out, to quote, 'I have fucking 550-odd bhp and I'm *still* beaten by a fuckin' Smart car.' And that would have been the title of this book, but for the obvious reason. One more award to go: the Spirit of the Cannonball, which went to Darren and Dean who made the journey by hook or by crook.

A photo-shoot was undertaken with us and our trophies and then it was back to the bar for a few more drinks and social inter-course. Depositing the trophy back in our room we headed off to the prearranged nightclub a few yards from the hotel and the party started to swing. Stories and drinks abounded, the party pushed on into the very early hours, and I bumped into a certain Ferrari driver looking a bit red in the face who explained that on the road to Calais they had got stopped for speeding after a good few miles racing the police at 175mph, at times, and the police calling in a helicopter to help. Having been stopped they were fined €10,000 to get their car back, which was returned when offered €750. The driver had his licence taken away but as he put it, all he would do would be to claim he has lost it and the DVLA would send him another one. The party carried on and as the club was emptying out a few of us were confronted by an angry clubber who wanted to sort us and the other bouncers out for the way we dealt with his mate. We aren't bouncers, we're Cannonballers in dinner suits! He walked away to find the bouncers.

Back to the hotel and, thankfully, the bar was still open. Champagne flowed and so did the wine, beer and vodka. Time marched on and a few of us decided to push on with a table-dancing club being mentioned. Once found, we knocked on the door to be told by a tired looking doorman that the club had closed an hour earlier. 'What time is it?'

'Ten past six mate,' came his reply.

*

Saturday morning was a long laborious affair with most drivers hanging around the foyer combining a lack of wanting the event to end with a serious lack of energy from the night before. We made our goodbyes and loaded the car for the last time. As we went to pull away we couldn't help noticing a certain Cannonballer driving off with one of the checkpoint girls!

After the drive back to Essex, the most sedate and uneventful of the previous six days, I dropped Adrian off and drove the five or so miles back home, pulled up on my drive, parked the Smart and headed in.

Monday morning came. Out I went and did what I have done numerous times in the past. Clicked the remote, got in the Smart, and driven it to work, something I have done every day since.

15

Now the Party's Over

After such an adventure you do have a come-down. Sunday proved that: the whole day passed with me feeling as if I had just awoken from a very deep sleep. Five days of hard driving and partying had caught up with me with a vengeance. The next couple of weeks drifted along with various people congratulating us and asking questions about what it had been like, and then I was put in touch with someone from Mercedes: remember them? They were one of the people who didn't get our leaflets nor returned my calls when looking for sponsorship. Anyway, they were interested in what the car had done and arranged for a photographer to meet Adrian and myself to get some promotional shots. A trip to 'Hey Guys' one Sunday morning preceded meeting up for the shoot which took place at High Beach, part of Epping Forest near to where we both live. Some really good shots of the car and ourselves were taken and the photographer kindly bought us a cup of tea and a chocolate biscuit out of his expenses – on Mercedes, of course. Ironically, when starting out on the whole venture, I immediately thought that on approaching Mercedes they would jump at the chance to get involved and throw good money at us to promote Smart in such a high-calibre race, especially bearing in mind the opposition. However in the real world all we got was a cup of tea and a KitKat each!

We appeared on quite a few Smart websites and a local paper did a full-page spread on us with a few more local magazines and free-bees mentioning us. Globally, in print, I am aware that we appeared in newspapers in Malaysia, New Zealand and Mississauga, which is

26 miles south of Toronto in Canada. As word spread we were mentioned on over 75 websites, appeared in *The Sun*, were voiced on half a dozen radio stations, and, to the immense pride of my boys and myself, appeared in *Nuts* magazine.

What of the sponsorship I wrote of earlier? Well, with the aid of the website, and general sponsorship, we raised about £1,700 for the NSPCC, which all helps. Oddly, on one website we had one person claiming we were ignorant raising money for that charity, who then went on for ages telling us why, and why we should be raising money for loads of other charities, plus some other character claiming we had copied his car!

As time passes between the finish and speeds to the next rally, interest in the car and the event doesn't seem to diminish at all. I'm still getting stopped and asked about the car and the website, zoom-zoomsmart, is still being hit more than the new site zzsracing.com. In March 2009 I received a phone call from a local kids' nursery asking if the Smart, not me, the Smart, could come and be at their fifth birthday celebration.

So what of the whole thing? If you're into cars and all things associated with them, then to participate in a Cannonball Run really ticks every box for you. The six days – five of driving and the rest partying and chatting to like-minded people – is definitely hard to beat. The other drivers were all people that you could spend time with and enjoy it. The camaraderie was excellent, a feeling of us against Europe, all of us with a common goal, and all of us respecting each other's cars and ideals. In a Smart we could have faced derision and scorn, bearing in mind that most drivers entered the event in a car worth around £60,000 plus and were faced with a little £7,000 car. However, not once did we encounter anything like that. Eighteen months after the event I'm still in touch with a few of the drivers and Jan, the organiser; drunken nights are still had in London, emails are frequently exchanged and banter on Facebook and Twitter etc. is still rife.

The whole exercise from day one, when the idea hatched, to the last day, was an education. It definitely proved that nothing was easy and that after all we went through, all the rejections of sponsorship, the people that came through were, in fact, the people we would want to be with.

They were:

smarts r us, the brilliant, helpful operation based in Nottingham who, in the early days, could have fleeced me for £s but didn't, instead offering 100 per cent honest and expert advice.

Hampstead Plumbing and Heating, a plumbing company based in Hampstead, North London, who immediately sponsored us to raise money for the NSPCC.

Hadleigh Residential estate agents based in Belsize Park, who again didn't hesitate to sponsor us.

LD Law, based in Harlow, Essex, a firm of solicitors with a big heart.

Fitzrovia Construction, situated in the West End of London, definitely weren't shy in sponsoring me.

Immage Worx of Harlow did the excellent graphics on the car.

Merecedes Benz, cheers for the tea and KitKat; well in fact, thanks to the photographer Warren who actually bought it.

To everyone else who kindly sponsored me a big big thank you.

So where did everyone finish? Have a look at Table 2.

Reading through the list of cars it does show the amazing calibre of the vehicles that participated, of which many will return in 2009, no doubt.

Will we?

Well I think you can guess that.

In the Smart?

No, the Smart has proved its point.

I could, bearing in mind the complete lack of interest shown by

Table 2

Position/Car		Driver	Driver	Final Variance from 61mph
1	Barbus Smart	Adrian Hull	David Ward	0.00
2	BMW 530D	Jamie Chapman	Anisa Aubin	0.01
3	Ford Mustang	Andrew Paul	Michael Lacey	0.05
4	Subaru Impreza	Adrian Howells	Kevin Hughes	0.08
5	BMW M3	Ray Ramnath	Graham Butler	0.11
6	Porsche 911	Andrew Jenkins	Stephen Potter	0.27
7	Porsche Boxter S	Alex Paterson	Scott Paterson	0.75
8	Ferrari 430	Derek Rogers	Will Price	1.20
9	Vauxhall Vectra	Darren Wilkinson	Dean Pappin	1.69
10	Porsche Carrera S 997	Simon Chaplin	Nick Fitch	1.82
11	Lamborghini	Kash Singh	Raj Kaur	1.98
12	Bentley Continental GT	Gary Ford	Nigel Schroder	2.51
13	Lotus Elise	Philip Green	Lisa Green	6.77
14	Ferrari 360	Rory Bell	Joseph Reynolds	6.96
15	Mazda RX7	Steve Callesa	Frank Spiteri	7.31
16	Porsche	Bruce Bourke	Craig Preston	8.27
17	TVR 350T	Kevin Wallwork	Robbie Catt	8.42
18	Honda S2000	Dean Taylor	Claire Taylor	8.45
19	Mitisbishi FQ300	Tom Richmond	Matt Yeomans	10.03
20	Audi S5	Danny Johnson	Kerry Tomlinson	11.12
21	Porsche 911	Chris Houghton	Mathew Sutcliffe	14.79
22	Maserati Granturismo	Luigi Pacelli	Joel Sadler	15.31
23	Aston Martin V8	Shane Smith	Sam Cowen	16.35
24	Audi RS6	Andy Rowe	Ashley Watt	24.85
25	BMW M5	Richard Hunt	Mathew Monks/ Chris Hinks	26.46
26	Ferrari 430 Spider F1	Dean Langton	Stuart Bell	26.94
27	BMW Z4m	Simon Fearnley	Nick Fearnley	28.35
28	BMW 530d Sport	Dave Collins	Mairead Higgins	32.66
29	Porsche 911	Jonathan Beeson	Daniel Beecroft	41.27
30	Audi RS6 Avant	Scott Lewis	Daniel Schofield	48.41
31	Corvette Z06	Paul Barker	Stuart Jones	49.59
32	Mini Cooper S	Jon Evans	Greg Evans	51.10
33	Ferrari 430	Carl Rolaston	Steve Smith	53.83
34	BMW 335	Rene Simoons	Patrick Altink	57.35

Table 2 – *continued*

Position/Car	Driver	Driver	Final Variance from 61mph
35 Mercedes GL500	Simon Worts	Ferdi Pacelli	68.04
36 Jaguar XKR	Neil Leggett	Mark Stewart	Did not finish
37 Lamborghini	Paul Naden	Shaynee Pitfield	Did not finish
38 Vauxhall VX220	Sam Rose	Colin Jennings	Did not finish

Mercedes and Brabus, slag off the car, but only if I could find anything to critisise about it. This little Brabus Smart took us round Europe averaging 61mph on the button; the only car in almost ten years of The Cannonball to achieve this. It impressed a British Touring car driver at the Estoril track causing him to declare it his highlight of the day; it touched 120mph and it is still used nearly every day of the week; it still causes numerous people to stare and smile; it still starts first time, stops when asked and occasionally, very occasionally, goes fast

What of 2009? The immediate reaction after 2008 was the sheer fun we had in an unconventional car for this event, so bear in mind that a roofless 1972 1600cc metallic purple Beach Buggy was bought from e-bay by a complete lunatic who picked the car up from its owner in Troon in Scotland and drove it 411 miles on a drizzly wet Wednesday afternoon back to Essex and into a garage where it will stay until the time cometh.

BE AFRAID, BE VERY AFRAID

THE END
(Yeah right!)

THE SMART ONE

I left my job, my boss, my car and my home
I'm leaving for a destination I still don't know
somewhere nobody must have duties at home
And if you like this, you can follow me
So let's go

Follow me
And let's go
To the place where we belong
and leave our troubles at home
Come with me
We can go
To a paradise of love and joy
A destination unknown

Now I won't feel those heavy duties no more
My life gets better now I finally enjoy
Yes all the people wanna come here and so
Come on and join us you can do that now
Let's go

Follow me
And let's go
To the place where we belong
and leave our troubles at home
Come with me
We can go
To a paradise of love and joy
A destination unknown

We left the city, the pollution, the crowd
The air is clear, the ocean's blue, I love that sound
we're happy for this destination we found
And if you want this, you can follow me
Let's go
Follow me
And let's go
To the place where we belong
and leave our troubles at home
Come with me
We can go to a paradise of love and joy
destination unknown.